The Nation's Top Programs

EXCELLENCE IN LIBRARY SERVICES TO YOUNG ADULTS

FOURTH EDITION

Young Adult Library Services Association

Renée Vaillancourt McGrath

Editor

AMERICAN LIBRARY ASSOCIATION
Chicago 2004

Design and composition by ALA Production Services

The paper used in this publication meets the minimum requirements of American National Standard for Information Sciences—Permanence of Paper for Printed Library Materials, ANSI Z39.48-1992

Printed in the United States of America

08 07 06 05 04   5 4 3 2 1

3/17   5613

Contents

8: Teen Advisory Boards

9: Young Adults with Disabilities

Acknowledgements

The contributions of many people combined to make this book possible.

The late Hardy Franklin, former director of the District of Columbia Public Library, inspired and obtained funding for the first *Excellence* book when he was president of the American Library Association in 1993–94.

The Margaret Edwards Trust has provided funding for each edition of *Excellence in Library Services to Young Adults* in keeping with Edwards' desire to promote the free reading of teenagers and young adults. The centennial edition of Edwards' seminal work, *The Fair Garden and the Swarm of Beasts* (ALA, 2002), commemorated what would have been Margaret Edwards' hundreth birthday.

Mary K. Chelton compiled and edited the first three editions of *Excellence in Library Services to Young Adults*. It has been an honor to walk in her footsteps.

Linda Waddle, former deputy executive director of YALSA, wrote the grant application for the fourth edition of *Excellence* and developed the grant and scoring sheets for this project. Since her retirement in 2002, she has been sorely missed.

YALSA staff members Nicole Gilbert and Esther Murphy managed the 2003 grant application process. Cindy Welch provided much support and guidance on the content of the fourth edition, and Julie Walker oversaw the entire project.

The following members of the YALSA Executive Committee spent many hours selecting twenty-five winners from the sixty-seven grant applications received in 2003:

- Audra Caplan, YALSA president and director, Harford County Library System, Belcamp, Md.

- David Mowery, YALSA vice president/president-elect and division chief, Central Library Youth Services, Brooklyn (N.Y.) Public Library

- Caryn Sipos, YALSA immediate past president and branch manager, Three Creeks Community Library, Vancouver, Wash.

- C. Allen Nichols, YALSA fiscal officer and director, Wadsworth-Ella M. Everhard Public Library, Wadsworth, Ohio

- Catherine Clancy, YALSA division councilor and branch manager, Boston Public Library, Honan-Allston Branch

And of course, this book would not have been possible without the contributions of the twenty-five award winners that are featured in this collection. I am grateful for their willingness to share their outstanding ideas for successful programs with the young adult library community.

Preface

As a YALSA Serving the Underserved trainer, I have presented dozens of training sessions on various aspects of young adult services across the United States. One of the most frequent requests that I receive is for good program ideas that work. *Excellence in Library Services to Young Adults* is a showcase of some of the best tried-and-tested programs in the country.

The Excellence in Library Services to Young Adults project was started by ALA past-president Hardy Franklin in 1993. All four rounds of the project have been funded by the Margaret Alexander Edwards Trust. Edwards was a well-known and innovative young adult services librarian at the Enoch Pratt Free Library in Baltimore, Maryland, for more than thirty years.

This fourth edition highlights the top twenty-five programs chosen through a YALSA grant application process in 2003. The top five program winners (indicated with a Top Five logo in this book) were awarded a stipend of $1,000 each. The other twenty winners received $250 each. The applications were judged on the basis of the following criteria:

■ The degree to which the program/service meets the needs of its community, particularly the young adult audience it serves.

■ The originality of the program/service (creative, innovative, unique).

■ The degree to which the program/service reflects the concepts identified in *New Directions for Library Service to Young Adults* (ALA, 2002).

■ The degree to which the program/service affects and improves service to young adults.

■ The quality of the program/service (well-planned, well-organized, well-implemented, and well-evaluated).

Readers of previous editions of the *Excellence in Library Services to Young Adults* books will notice several changes in this edition. The first three editions divided chapters into the categories of programs/services listed on the grant application (see appendix B). The categories for the 2003–2004 grants were:

■ Information services—reference, access to information, resources sharing, technology, library orientations, information literacy instruction, information-seeking behavior enhancement.

■ Reading promotion—reader's advisory, book discussion groups, programs, displays, summer reading clubs.

■ Youth participation—decision-making, policy development, advisory groups.

■ Collaborative efforts—school/public library/university or college cooperation, community outreach coalitions.

■ Education support—tutoring, homework centers, instructional strategies.

■ Staff and volunteer development—in-service training, mentoring, instruction.

■ Intergenerational—planned opportunities for different age groups to interact with one another.

■ Special needs—meeting the special needs of young adults with physical, mental, learning, or emotional disabilities or in special facilities, such as hospitals, homeless shelters.

■ Teen Read Week—activities, promotion, publicity.

These categories reflect many of the principles presented in *New Directions for Library Service to Young Adults* and are important elements to include in young adult library programs. However, since many of the award-winning grants included several of the components listed above, chapter headings that were more descriptive of the ultimate goal of the programs were created to assist readers in finding information about the specific types of programs that they are interested in. The categories chosen for chapter headers in this edition are:

- After-school programs—activities designed to provide young adults with productive ways to spend out-of-school hours.

- Career preparation—programs that provide work-related skills or introduce teens to a particular career.

- Creative expression—projects designed to encourage and showcase the creativity of teens.

- Life skills—workshops that provide information or training in areas that will help teens grow into successful adults.

- Literary appreciation—innovative activities that encourage a love of literature.

- Miscellany—programs that meet the needs of particular young adult populations or library staff.

- Young adults with disabilities—services that address the needs of teens with physical, mental, learning, or emotional disabilities.

- Summer reading—programs that promote, present, or follow up on young adult summer reading activities.

- Teen advisory boards—groups that involve teens in planning, promoting, or providing library services.

Chapters are organized in alphabetical order, as are the programs featured within each chapter. In addition to the updated chapter headings, this edition of *Excellence in Library Services to Young Adults* also introduces a new format for the presentation of information within each entry. Each program is listed first by the program name, then by the name and location of the sponsoring institution. The sections included within each program are as follows:

- Target audience—the age and specific characteristics of the population for which the program is designed.

- Program description—a brief overview of the essential components of the program.

- Sponsoring institution—information about the library or school that sponsored the program as well as any partnering agencies.

- Young adult demographics—the socioeconomic characteristics of the community, with particular focus on the teen population.

- Program participants—numbers and more in-depth description of the teens (or library staff members) who attended the program or participated in program activities.

- Youth participation—the degree to which young adults were involved in the planning, promotion, and evaluation of the program or service.

- Staff and volunteers—the number of paid staff and volunteers required to run the program.

- Budget—the cost (including staff time and materials) of the program and funding sources.

- Evaluation—how was the program evaluated, and what was learned from the evaluation process.

- Impact of the program—more detailed description of the program, emphasizing the ways that it made a difference in the lives of young adults (outcomes).

- For more information—the grant applicant and contact person for the program.

This redesign in structure was intended to make it easier for readers to browse through the book to find program ideas that would be suitable for their particular young adult populations. However, the intent of this book is not to provide packaged programs that readers can duplicate. Rather, the concepts and ideas behind each of these programs can serve as an inspiration for readers to create new programs that are uniquely suited to the needs of the young adults in their own communities.

The programs featured in this book range from inexpensive, one-time events sponsored by small public libraries or school library media centers, to more expensive and elaborate on-going services with numerous community partners and outside funding sources. Readers should not be discouraged by libraries that have greater staff or financial resources than their own. Several of the programs featured in this book were conducted by only one staff member with minimal funding from the library budget. Some of the more elaborate programs may be able to be modified in order to significantly cut costs as well. Readers should feel free to borrow elements from the various programs presented here and combine them with input from local teens to make them their own.

My hope is that the programs presented in this edition of *Excellence in Library Services to Young Adults* will inspire readers to create new and better young adult programs.

Introduction

The fourth edition of *Excellence in Library Services to Young Adults* began on the tenth anniversary of the beginning of the program in 1993, which happens to be the year that I graduated from the Catholic University of America with an MSLS funded by a Department of Education Title IIB Scholarship for Young Adult Services. The past decade has brought significant progress in the field of young adult services. When I was in library school there were only a handful of librarians who would even consider working with teenagers in libraries. Today there are a growing number of young, hip (and sometimes not-so-young or -hip) librarians who are excited about the possibility of working with this challenging and dynamic age group. Library administrators are also becoming increasingly aware of the need to provide spaces and services for young adults in libraries.

Although no recent studies have been done about the number of young adult librarians in public libraries, many library systems are acknowledging the importance of serving teenagers by creating young adult areas staffed by young adult librarians and often designed with teen input. More and more libraries and schools are also developing teen advisory boards to advise staff on young adult collection development and programming decisions. Electronic discussion lists for young adult and secondary school librarians have proliferated and provide an open forum for the exchange of ideas within the field.

Membership in the Young Adult Library Services Association (YALSA) has doubled in the past ten years as the association has developed innovative training programs and partnered with large corporations and nonprofits to gather information about the reading interests of teens and to promote awareness-building activities, such as Teen Read Week.

YALSA's Serving the Underserved program, designed to teach young adult librarians how to educate generalists about the needs of young adults in libraries, has trained ninety librarians in how to conduct young adult professional development workshops. Approximately sixty-six of these trainers remain active in twenty-six states and have reached more than twenty thousand program participants. The list of available trainers can be found on the YALSA Web site at www.ala.org/yalsa under "Professional Development."

Over the course of the past decade, librarians have become more aware of the youth development movement in other youth-serving agencies that emphasizes the importance of involving teens (and even younger children) in all levels of decision-making that will affect the services provided for (and by) them. Organizations such as the Search Institute (www.search-institute.org) have conducted research that shows that children and teenagers need certain internal and external assets (also referred to in other models as inputs, or resiliency factors) in order to grow into healthy, successful, contributing adult members of society. The publication of *New Directions for Library Service to Young Adults* formally introduces these concepts into young adult library services and proposes a new model for working with young adults in libraries.

The programs selected for inclusion in this edition of *Excellence in Library Services to Young Adults* reflect this new direction in young adult services. All of the top programs go beyond the traditional role of the library to respond to the comprehensive needs of young adults in their respective service communities. Many of these programs involve community partnerships to ensure that young adults receive the type of information and support that they need on a variety of different levels. The programs are specifically designed to address the demographics of the service population, and are often multifaceted, on-going services rather than one-time-only events. Young adults are involved at all levels in the planning, presentation, and evaluation of the best programs, and the success of these programs can be measured as much by the impact that the program has on the lives of teens (outcomes) as by the number of young adults who participate (outputs).

It is an exciting time to be working with teenagers in libraries. The programs described in this book show how libraries are making a difference in the lives of teenagers across the United States. I hope these ideas will inspire other young adult librarians to reach new heights of excellence.

1. After-School Programs

Studies have shown that teens who participate in supervised activities during after-school hours are less likely to get into trouble. These two after-school programs provide multifaceted library- and community-based activities designed to meet the particular needs of the low-income and at-risk residents of these two communities. Both involve youth in the design of the programs and feature library/community agency partnerships. One is highly structured and well-funded, while the other manages to accomplish many of the same goals with more modest means. The variety of activities provided in these after-school programs are sure to draw teens into the library and keep them coming back.

Kearns Library Teen Program

Salt Lake County Library Services, Kearns, Utah

Target Audience

At-risk junior high students

Program Description

The Kearns branch of the Salt Lake County Library Services (SLCLS) and the Salt Lake County Division of Youth Services (SLCDYS) team up to provide a special teen program every Thursday afternoon at Kearns Library. About seventy-five to one hundred youth descend en masse on the library daily after school. They are a diverse, low-income, multicultural, high-risk group of kids who spend several hours every day hanging out. The program's purpose is to educate and entertain youth in grades six through twelve with activities geared to their interest level while introducing the library and other government resources to promote positive citizenship and lasting values. This is accom-

plished through a series of after-school lectures, skills demonstrations, field trips, and hands-on workshops.

A primary objective of the program is to improve the teens' behavior while providing them with positive experiences, a variety of role models, and a wide range of opportunities. Using community members, retired volunteers, and media experts, the program allows teens to help plan and present library programs. It has proven that these trouble kids are amazing individuals who respond well to positive adult interaction and approval.

Sponsoring Institution

Kearns Library is one of eighteen public SLCLS libraries. SLCLS serves more than 900,000 residents living in diverse cities, communities, and neighborhoods spanning a 764-square-mile area. SLCLS's mission is to make a positive difference in people's lives, wherever they may live in Salt Lake County, by offering them convenient access to services and materials for both information and recreation.

Located in southwestern Salt Lake County, Kearns Library is considered a family library characterized by a diverse collection of more than 104,000 items. In addition to books and audio and video collections, Kearns offers patrons fourteen personal computers with free Internet access. The computers are extremely popular with teen patrons and are in constant use from after school to closing time.

SLCDYS teamed up with the Kearns Library to make this program possible.

Young Adult Demographics

Kearns Junior High School (KJHS) has a population of 1,100 students—560 young men and 519 young women. The population breaks down to 69 percent Caucasian, 22 percent Hispanic, and 9 percent Asian, Pacific Islander, Native American, and African-American.

The school test scores indicate the level of help that is needed for these kids. The 2001 SAT composite score for KJHS eighth-graders was 32. The expected range

Several woodcutters and a group of teens.

was 34 to 59. The Utah composite score was 56, and the national composite score was 50. These are mostly low-income kids without the resources to take extra classes or to participate in recreational activities, such as sports and dance.

Program Participants

Students from KJHS, which is located across a field from Kearns Library, are the target audience of the teen program. For more than forty years students from this school have congregated every day at the library. In the past few years, the situation had become intolerable. Student behavior was rude, offensive, dangerous, and, in some cases, illegal. The staff and patrons had to deal with vandalism, graffiti, illegal skateboarding on sidewalks and stairs, physical intimidation, blocking of access to the library, fighting, and abusive name calling in several languages. Police were often called to the library to stop fights and remove students.

All teens are welcome to participate in the program, but the vast majority of participants consist of the eighty to one hundred junior high school students who enter the library daily and stay for at least an hour and sometimes two or three. On average, twenty to forty students participate in each activity. However, depending on the activity, different groups of students may be involved. An estimated one hundred students have participated in the program at one time or another.

Youth Participation

The program was started by holding a brainstorming session with a group of teens. The teens suggested activities that could be offered. A survey that incorporated their ideas was developed and administered to the youth as a whole to assess their interest in various activities. The most appealing activities were then planned and scheduled. Teens continue to approach library staff with new activity ideas, which are accommodated whenever possible. As a result of the recently established teen advisory board, young adults are now taking a more active and formal role in program planning, development, and evaluation.

Staff and Volunteers

The teen program is conducted with very little staff involvement. One librarian does most of the planning and supervising, while the manager provides backup and a lot of ideas and phone support. There are generally two people from SLCDYS present at activities—an employee and an intern—but occasionally only one can attend the program.

Budget

The program had little funding until Wal-Mart donated $1,000. SLCDYS has donated food, some transportation, and harmonicas. Kearns Library has about $200 available for supplies, which is used to provide materials for crafts. Volunteer program presenters also often donate supplies for their particular activities. Library staff time equates to approximately $35 per week—one librarian paid at $17 per hour, working approximately two hours per week on the teen program. SLCDYS interns are not paid, and the SLCDYS employee, who works approximately one hour per week, is paid approximately $15 per hour. Other program funding and expenditures include a $100 speaker's fee paid by the Utah Humanities Foundation for a presentation at the library on children's media.

Evaluation

A survey was administered to see how participants felt about the teen program, determine whether it should be continued, and solicit ideas for future programs and activities. The results were overwhelmingly positive. Overall, the teen program at Kearns Library has been very successful in meeting the immediate need of solving a severe problem. In addition, the program has become an important factor in the lives of those who participate in it. Because the teen program has been so beneficial to not only teens, but to members of the Kearns staff and the community, the library intends to continue the program for many years to come.

Impact of the Program

The teen program at Kearns Library became increasingly more important as it grew and developed during the first year. What was initially a trial experiment now has a future. This special group of teens does not always have access to supportive home environments or extracurricular activities. Junior high school students also have a strong need to socialize as groups in a safe area. Although the library has previously tried to meet the teens' needs, the financial or human resources were not previously available to develop and manage a structured program. Partnering with SLCDYS provided the monetary and staff help that was needed to plan and organize the teen program.

The program's facilitators are SLCDYS interns—graduate students enrolled in the University of Utah's social work program. Some program activities, such as trips to a skateboard park, are designed just for fun, while others have a dual purpose of entertaining and educating youth. For example, members of the Utah National Guard provided a climbing wall and at the same time presented a drug education program. Seventy-five students participated in that activity.

In addition to educating and entertaining the teens, the program offers them the opportunity to interact with adult role models of various ages and backgrounds. For example, a reporter from a major daily newspaper wrote a story about the teen program at Kearns Library, then later returned to speak to the youth about his career. Another after-school activity was woodcarving, presented by eight local carvers between the ages of sixty-five and eighty who visited with the kids while teaching them to carve soapstone with files. Forty-six students participated in that program; the activity was so popular that half of the participants returned for a second session even though it coincided with the first day of spring break.

Harmonica instruction was another intergenerational activity that was extremely popular with the teens. A local retired man heard about the teen program at Kearns and volunteered to teach the kids to play the harmonica. If the students attended three lessons, they could keep the harmonicas, which were donated by SLCDYS. Twenty-seven kids were rewarded with harmonicas as well as an enriching experience with an interesting gentleman.

The students' positive reactions to the teen program shows that they are developing the assets they need to be successful. For many kids, the teen program is the only after-school activity available to them. The students are developing open and honest relationships with the adult facilitators as they realize that they will not be judged or graded on their interactions. As a result, teens now come and ask for help and offer to help out at the library. A teen advisory board that encourages its members to plan and produce most of the programs has been formed. Its members are learning leadership, group interaction, and other life skills.

The teens are also taking ownership in the library, learning to respect it as an important place in their lives and in the community. Students now take responsibility for their own behavior; there have not been any recent

fights on library property or during program activities. The kids are also beginning to realize that the community cares about them. A karate business conducted a martial arts demonstration then donated headbands and free lessons to the kids. After hearing about the teen program, a local Wal-Mart donated $1,000 to support it.

The teens are now asking for more activities, and they are willing to help plan and carry them out. They want to start a book club and create their own displays in the young adult area. They also want art contests, and they have volunteered to be in the local parade as the library entry. Yu-Gi-Oh and chess tournaments have also been popular.

Has the program made a difference? Absolutely. Patrons are no longer afraid to enter the library, kids are respectful and behave much better, staff members are less stressed, and the library and SLCDYS staff members are making some amazing new friends. Most of all, everyone who participates is having fun. The students who participate in this program are future bond voters and leaders. They deserve respect, help, and friendship. The area's low test scores indicate that adults need to help these youth in any way they can so that the community will have an educated, informed, and successful new generation growing up. These are kids that can easily be on the streets instead of in the library. We want them at Kearns.

For More Information

Darlene Dineen
Library Manager
Kearns Library
5350 S. 4220 W.
Kearns, UT 84118
(801) 944-7612
(801) 967-8958 (fax)
ddineen@slco.lib.ut.us

TIGERS

Franklin County Public Library/Friends of the Franklin County Public Library, Eastpoint, Fla.

Target Audience

At-risk middle, junior high, and senior high school students

Program Description

Teens in Gear Enjoy, Realize, Succeed (TIGERS) is a multifaceted, library-based after-school program that provides services designed to develop, individualize, and further the long-range plans of Franklin County youth. The goal of TIGERS is to break negative cycles of undereducation, family turmoil, poverty, and teen pregnancy by offering positive, enriching, educational activities that enhance both individual growth and employability of participants.

Young adults each achieve a minimum of one individualized goal in a one-year period of time through carefully designed, success-oriented projects that focus on reading, academic development, public speaking, resiliency, art enrichment, internships, and work readiness.

Funded by a grant from the Gulf Coast Workforce Board, TIGERS is held weekdays at Apalachicola Program Center and the Eastpoint and Carrabelle branches of Franklin County Public Library (FCPL). Conducting the TIGERS program at FCPL increases library use among teens and inspires lifelong learning.

Sponsoring Institution

Prior to 1992, Franklin County did not have a public library. The many obstacles to healthy family life in a diverse rural environment necessitated a community-focused library service. From its inception, the library's mission moved beyond the traditional and incorporated a dedication to breaking negative lifestyles. The library's phenomenal growth—a new building, a small branch, and a program center—is the direct result of providing a host of specialized youth and family projects.

The Friends of the Franklin County Public Library (FFCPL) has played a major role in the library's history and continuing development. The library's initial existence was made possible by FFCPL joining forces with Wakulla and Jefferson Public Libraries to form the cooperative Wilderness Coast Public Libraries. FFCPL support ranges from supplementing basic operating costs, to raising matching construction grant funds, to serving as fiscal agent for a variety of grant-funded projects, including TIGERS.

Young Adult Demographics

In order to understand teen demographics in this community, it is essential to view the county as a whole unit. Franklin County is a rural, panhandle fishing community with a population of 10,872 (86.7 percent Caucasian, 12.4 percent African-American, 5.2 percent Hispanic) according to the 2000 *Florida Literacy Data and Statistics Handbook* (Florida Literacy Coalition, 2000). Recreational activities are few to none. Traditional economic systems reliant on small family fishing industries are clashing with a new and skyrocketing tourist consumer economy, creating a need for new kinds of job skills training. There are three primary neighborhoods, two middle/high schools (both received a 2002 Department of Education grade "C"

rank), one elementary school in each community, a new charter school, and 1,368 registered public school students. The county has a 41 percent functional illiteracy rate—27 percent at lowest level, according to the 2002 *Florida Literacy Data and Statistics Handbook*. The School Accountability Report shows below state-minimum performance criteria; college entry test results are below state average in all categories. The county ranks twenty-sixth in state unemployment according to the 2002 data from the Florida Agency for Workforce Innovation, and 80 percent of students qualify for free lunch according to the 2002 Federal Communication Commission. Poverty and undereducation perpetuate negative family environments contributing to juvenile delinquency, truancy, drug use, teen pregnancy, and abuse. The *Florida Youth Substance Abuse Survey* (Florida Department of Children and Families, 2002) reports that Franklin County youth ages ten to seventeen engaged in higher than state average delinquency behavior, and drug use is also higher than the state average. Current State Library of Florida risk indicators show a 25.7 percent birth rate to teenagers; Franklin County Health Department Indicator Data 2001 shows that 80 percent of teen mothers are unwed.

Program Participants

TIGERS participants are primarily twelve- to eighteen-year-olds with risk factors encompassing, but not limited to, low income, truancy, undereducation, and family instability. Staff and students work together on a goal achievement contract. All students fourteen and older receive career aptitude screening, academic assessment, and the option of performance-based internships based on determined direction. TIGERS has served 319 cumulative students and continues to work intensely with 165 youth.

Youth Participation

Tri-Site Teen Council meetings are conducted quarterly to instill program unity and to afford youth an opportunity to update project direction. TIGERS participants are encouraged to give back to the community by taking part in county cleanups, visiting nursing homes, and participating in service organization fundraisers and special events. They also make presentations at local council meetings, and one student received first place in the state for a PEACE poster contest.

Career development and cultural enrichment field trips are provided based on interest and determined need. Many students have never traveled any distance, and most have not had the opportunity to attend plays, concerts, and museums. Students have received a behind-the-scenes tour of Gulf World and had an opportunity to swim with the dolphins. They also attended the Seaside International Ballet, Florida State University's Seven Days of Opening Nights, Mission St.

WING IT!!!

Spring 2001 WINGS/TIGERS
Franklin County Public Library.

The *official* art and literary 'Zine of the Franklin County WINGS/TIGERS program.

The goal of WINGS/TIGERS is to provide positive, enriching, educational and cultural activities which will inspire individual growth and increase awareness, self-esteem, life skills, career development, and employability or future employability of participants.

Luis, the Nat King Cole Musical Trip, IMAX flight simulation, and ROPES course team training. All students write field trip and special activity reports. Despite some expressing fear initially about being away from home, students have shown a tremendous appreciation for the trip opportunities and how they have changed their lives. The level of writing, self-expression, spirit of teamwork, and interest in reading has increased dramatically since the beginning of the TIGERS program.

Staff and Volunteers

Three full-time coordinators and three part-time staff members share the caseload of students. In addition, TIGERS staff consists of a part-time project director to oversee and fiscally manage the program and a part-time administrative assistant. Two library staff, two literacy program staff, one Experience Works assistant, four community volunteers, and interagency partner guest speakers provide regular services as needed. Partners sometimes include Franklin County schools and health agencies, Capital City Youth Services, Refuge House, Early Head Start, and Franklin's Promise.

Budget

Library locations are fully equipped with materials, educational resources, and state-of-the-art computers provided by the Franklin County Board of County Commissioners general operating budget, which includes county funds, local donations, FFCPL funding, State Aid to Libraries, and such additional funding sources as the Gates Library Foundation.

Program-specific expenses are made possible by Federal Welfare in Action (WIA) and Welfare Transition (WT) funds contracted through the Gulf Coast Workforce Board. The current TIGERS grant funding budget is $300,972 ($100,000 WT/$200,972 WIA):

5.5 FTE staff salaries and benefits	$172,458
Supplies	$1,162
Rent	$2,250
Utilities	$174
Communications	$1,521
Postage	$180
Training and travel	$2,400
Field trips	$22,094
Advertising	$60.00
Internships	$91,030
Student bonuses/expenses	$2,670
Participant insurance	$2,000
Meeting expenses	$973
Administrative/audit	$2,000

Evaluation

The strength of the young adult library program has been its ability to grow and change in order to meet the needs of the youth in the community. The TIGERS program provides consistency, staff accessibility, total youth involvement, performance-based training, enrichment activities, tutoring, homework assistance, basic and life skills development, and field trips.

At the close of the program year in June 2002, there were 201 students on board and 289 projects provided. Students were monitored, and reports were conducted on all activities, youth development, and goal achievement. Ninety-nine precent of all goals were attained. Seven students graduated high school, and of them five went to college and one went into the Navy. Four students who dropped out of school during this period attained their GED. All students who exited the program were put on follow-up coordinator contact services. There was a 98 percent positive contact rate. As of May 2003, 319 students have been served and 332 projects were provided for students cumulatively. Nine students will be graduating, with two receiving their GED. All students exiting the program have achieved at least one goal.

Overall, youth participation in the library has increased notably. Students are reading books, using computers, and accessing library resources. Youth attending library programs traditionally become readers

TIGERS

TEENS IN GEAR!

at the
Franklin County
Public Library

ON THE MOVE

FCPL is reaching out into the community's youth, offering a special library section, a special program, books of interest to young adults, and a team of dedicated adults to provide consistent and genuine positive reinforcement. In this way, the library is providing services that will ultimately inspire lifelong learning, library use, and future generations of library advocates.

Impact of the Program

Responding to a need for youth programs in Franklin County, the library received a Juvenile Justice Community Partnership Grant in 1994. WINGS—denoting growth and soaring—operated three program sites in the major communities providing year-round after-school programs for teens. WINGS was designed according to determined need, youth voice in program development, interagency partner input, and constant evaluation. During the first year of operation (the public library was only two years old), parents who were not accustomed to having a library in the community expressed great concern about where their children were going after school. WINGS received recognition, and was selected by the American Library Association and listed in *Excellence in Library Services to Young Adults* (ALA, 1997) as being one of the top five library programs for youth in the nation.

Although WINGS has continued to be a highly successful and productive library project for nine consecutive years, decreased funding and the ability to satisfy the growing needs of youth became drastically limited, in particular for the older teen group. In order to increase services, the library applied for and received a pilot grant from the Gulf Coast Workforce Board. TIGERS began in January 2000 as an enhancement to the WINGS program. Modeled after WINGS and working in conjunction with the existing program but going beyond program cutbacks, TIGERS sparked new enthusiasm and provided an additional thirty weekly program hours. Activities were linked to encompass heightened basic skills training, field trips, guest speakers, teen pregnancy prevention activities, career and life skills development, and academic achievement. Through a carefully designed individualized planning contract, participants were offered an opportunity to explore future options and receive assistance in meeting both short- and long-term goals. The collaborative blending of the two youth projects is best described by a poster created by a student: "TIGERS—Without WINGS You Can't Fly," and the continuation of the popular *WING-IT!!* magazine.

In April 2003, FCPL was the recipient of the prestigious Florida Library Association's 2003 Betty Davis Miller Youth Services Award presented for an outstanding and distinctive young adult library program. The TIGERS program was commended for its spirit of teamwork and dedication; the library was applauded for being truly on a mission.

and future library users—many are first-generation library users. Library customers and volunteers have commented that previous youth members—the over-twenty-year-olds—who they meet in the everyday world are quick to state that they were once part of the program. Youth records indicate a developing level of self-awareness and understanding of responsibility. This serves to increase self-esteem, offer a window of opportunity, and provide hope for the future. Youth continue to be counseled to understand the importance of making educated, safe, responsible life choices.

TIGERS is an essential community asset that responds to the needs of its youth and the traditionally underserved library population. Working with a small number of peers in the comfortable, nonthreatening library environment with materials geared toward teen interest provides positive results.

Students take part in public speaking activities and currently are developing an extremely polished Poetry Slam series. Newsletters created by students are circulated throughout the county. Staff has developed a comprehensive Resiliency program based on the ADVANCE training system, which uses feature films to teach resiliency skills. One-hundred-and-thirteen students have received performance-based job shadowing internships relative to determined goals. Teen pregnancy prevention, responsible fatherhood, and parenting projects emphasize responsibility.

For More Information

Eileen Annie Ball
Library Director
Franklin County Public Library
P.O. Box 722
Eastpoint, FL 32328
(850) 670-8151
(850) 670-8151 (fax)
fcpl9@gtcom.net

2. Career Preparation

The two winning entries in this category take significantly different approaches to preparing teens for future careers. The Community Youth Corps is a comprehensive service learning program funded by a generous grant from Wallace-Reader's Digest funds and designed (with lots of youth input) to meet the needs of large groups of students. Job Shadow Day targets a smaller group of students who are interested in exploring a career in librarianship, thereby helping to address the librarian shortage that is anticipated as the baby boom generation retires. Both programs provide teens with important information and skills to prepare them for the workforce.

Community Youth Corps

Enoch Pratt Free Library, Baltimore, Md.

Target Audience

Middle, junior high, and senior high school students, including at-risk youth

Program Description

The Enoch Pratt Free Library's Community Youth Corps (CYC) was developed in 1999 with funding from the Wallace-Reader's Digest Funds. CYC's primary focus is to provide high-quality service learning and work experiences for Baltimore City young people and to expand Enoch Pratt Free Library's capacity to involve more teenagers in its program planning and implementation. Since its inception, CYC has trained more than two hundred young people in customer service, information literacy, library services, and media technology. In 2002–2003, CYC recruited seventy-five youth, provided year-long training and activities for them, and assisted them to gain valuable work and interpersonal skills. CYC's ultimate goal is to help city teenagers meet the challenges of adolescence and to prepare them for adulthood by providing a continuum of challenging positive activities, supportive adult attention, and opportunities to develop competence and confidence in their own innate abilities.

Sponsoring Institution

The mission of Pratt Library is to provide equal access to information and services that support, empower, and enrich all who pursue knowledge, education, cultural enrichment, and lifelong learning. Inherent in all that Pratt does is its commitment to helping Baltimore citizens improve their quality of life.

Pratt is a community-based system of branches and a central library. It was established in 1882 to provide library service to the residents of Baltimore, which today includes large populations of African-Americans, Hispanics, and Asians. The changing demographics and needs of the local community strongly influence the library's organizational goals and the types of programs they offer. In Baltimore City, with its high proportion of economically challenged residents, Pratt is often the only source of free educational and cultural programming available.

Young Adult Demographics

In Baltimore City, 24.8 percent of the population is younger than eighteen years of age (according to the 2000 census, the total population of Baltimore City is 651,154). Of these, 77.6 percent under eighteen are African-American and 1.9 percent are Hispanic. More than 34 percent of city children of all ages live in poverty as defined by the U.S. Poverty Threshold. More than 119,000 city children live in high-poverty neighborhoods.

The city has a high school dropout rate of more than 10 percent, and only 48.7 percent of high school graduates meet the minimum requirements for the University of Maryland system. Baltimore City also has the highest juvenile violent crime arrest rate in the state. These statistics were gathered from *Kids Count 2001,* a project of the Maryland Kids Count Partnership.

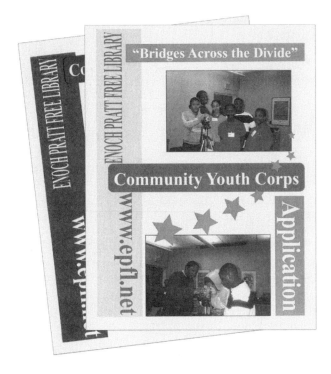

Program Participants

CYC serves teens from Baltimore, Maryland, middle and high schools, ages thirteen to fifteen. All teens are encouraged to apply for the program, which serves approximately seventy-five to one hundred students per year. The program is promoted in Pratt library branches throughout the city and through youth counselors in schools and recreational programs.

Youth Participation

CYC's ultimate purpose is to integrate as much youth involvement as possible in all areas of project design and implementation. Towards that end, CYC participants are used as consultants on all project activities. (The CYC program was, in fact, developed based on the findings of youth focus groups.) Pratt's teen summer reading program has comletely changed based on youth input. Youth create printed materials for the program, determine prize incentives for completing reading requirements, and develop programming. CYC teens also play an important role in summer reading program activities for younger children in that they assist librarians in Pratt branch libraries to implement programs, run informal story times, and ensure that all children coming to the branches are welcomed and assisted.

Staff and Volunteers

CYC involves ten library staff members and twelve volunteers. The program is led by Pratt's youth services coordinator, Asia Ali-Lunn, who has professional qualifications in programs serving young adults. Ali-Lunn is a relative newcomer to CYC, as she has only recently taken the place of the program's founding coordinator, Eric Rowe. Although not a librarian, Ali-Lunn works closely with Pratt's young adult library staff, especially its coordinator of school and student services, Deborah Taylor.

CYC also engages a core of college work-study students from Morgan State University and other area colleges as well as Americorps volunteers, who provide the teens with important near-peer role models. These volunteers are encouraged to work together with CYC teens, provide mentorship, and model positive social interactions.

Budget

CYC was originally funded through a three-year, $400,000 grant from the Wallace-Reader's Digest Funds. The term of the grant was completed in October 2002. Recognizing the importance of CYC to the youth of Baltimore, Pratt's leadership decided to keep the program as a part of the library's on-going initiatives. Currently, the program's $231,000 annual budget is defrayed through a combination of public/private sources. Just over half of the total budget ($126,050) is staff time and fringe, which is calculated based on the amount of time a staff member spends on CYC-specific activities multiplied by the individual's salary. The remaining $104,950 defrays direct expenses, which include stipends for participants who have completed their service-learning requirements, transportation costs for students and volunteers, programs costs, incentives for participants, and other direct costs. (We have found that the stipends and transportation costs are particularly important to keep teens involved in the program given the economic challenges facing so many Baltimore families.) Private support for CYC during 2002–2003 has come from the Baltimore Community Foundation, Mercantile Safe-Deposit and Trust, Verizon Foundation, the Helena Foundation, and Clayton Baker Trust.

Evaluation

Ongoing program evaluation is a part of all CYC activities. We ask teens to assess the strengths and weaknesses of the programs they design and participate in in an effort to teach them to think critically about their efforts. Parents and caregivers are asked to evaluate the impact the program has on their teenagers. Public participants at specific programs are also asked to evaluate the activities. All of this evaluative data is shared, discussed, and used to enhance future programming. Pratt's library staff have also been involved in extensive critical analysis of CYC's strengths and weaknesses as part of the library's participation in the Wallace-Reader's Digest Funds initiative. The lessons we have learned from our own analysis, plus the experiences of other grantees, have helped shape Pratt's CYC program.

Impact of the Program

CYC was developed by Pratt in an effort to move away from short-term, program-by-program planning for young adult services and move toward a comprehensive investment in youth services for the city of Baltimore. It was originally designed to address the need for youth-led library programs in response to the Wallace-Reader's Digest Funds' Public Libraries as Partners in Youth Development, a program designed to help library systems, particularly those in such urban low-income communities as Baltimore, develop high-quality education and career development programs for young people. Pratt was one of only nine libraries to receive an award under this initiative. Currently, CYC is one of only a handful of programs in the city that is designed to provide teenagers with opportunities to earn the service learning credits required for high school graduation in Maryland. In this way, the program also focuses its activities around a very real community need.

In keeping with the tenets of service learning (preparation, action, and reflection), Pratt staff have developed interactive journals as a part of the CYC experience. Through the act of journal keeping, students gain valuable insight throughout their CYC experience on how and why their service activities are meaningful.

In addition to providing after-school and summer learning activities that help students fulfill the service learning requirement, CYC also provides teens with opportunities to learn how to use information technology, practice interpersonal skills in an accepting environment, and gain work-related skills while working side-by-side with mentoring adult role models.

As a youth-centered program, CYC makes a very real difference in the lives of the young adults participating in the program. Through CYC, teens have a voice in program development and implementation at Pratt Library. In 2002, for example, CYC teens were instrumental in the success of Pratt's teen summer reading program and played an essential role in the successful completion of the library's summer reading program for preschool and elementary school children. CYC youth served as aides at the Pratt Center for Technology Training, and as homework helpers in branch libraries. Pratt also partnered with Wide Angle Media, a community-based organization that focuses on media literacy and video production, to provide specialized technology training for CYC students. Wide Angle Media instructors taught classes in media production to our teens, where they gained such skills as scriptwriting, storyboarding, and videography. At the end of each eight-week class, participants hosted a screening of their videos at the library.

Seventeen CYC participants received paid positions as a result of their involvement with CYC. Fourteen were hired by Youth Works, the city's summer employment program, and Pratt employed three CYC graduates to work in our summer reading outreach program.

CYC has invigorated young adult services at Pratt. It is a direct outgrowth of the library's strategic planning process, which, in the 1990s, recognized that reaching urban teens, many of them with low literacy levels, was a particular challenge. CYC has helped distinguish Pratt as one part of the home/school/community web of support necessary for strong youth development. CYC's emphasis on service learning has also provided the city school system with a meaningful alternative to school-based projects, many of which are difficult for teachers to manage, and offered parents and caregivers an opportunity to work together with the schools and the library to promote and celebrate teen achievement.

CYC has also brought new attention to Pratt on a local, regional, and national level. As a participant in the Wallace-Reader's Digest Funds Public Libraries As Partners in Youth Development Initiative, Pratt staff had the opportunity to meet and work with other library staff from all over the United States. CYC teens were a part of media promotion for the library's 2002 teen summer reading program, and the success of the program to date has helped the Pratt broaden its private sector funding.

For More Information

Deborah Taylor
Enoch Pratt Free Library
400 Cathedral St.
Baltimore, MD 21201
(410) 396-5356
(410) 396-1095 (fax)
dtaylor@epfl.net

Job Shadow Day

Cleveland Heights-University Heights (Ohio) Public Library

Target Audience

Senior high school students

Program Description

Cleveland Heights-University Heights (Ohio) Public Library (CHUHPL) hosted a Job Shadow Day during National Library Week in April 2002.

Designed to introduce high school students to library work, this four-hour pilot program was hosted by our young adult services coordinator. The program opened with an icebreaker featuring unexpected tasks done by librarians. A fast-paced recruitment video produced by the Ohio Library Council then set the tone for a presentation titled "It's Not Your Mother's Library Anymore." Afterwards, our human resources coordinator talked about library jobs and offered tips for filling out an application. A diverse staff panel convened to talk about their work and why they love their jobs. During a break, trivia contest winners were awarded chocolate. The highlight of the program was the opportunity for shadowing and hands-on work in one of six departments. Finally, students gathered to share their experiences during lunch with staff. Certificates of participation were distributed to all who attended.

Sponsoring Institution

CHUHPL serves two ethnically, culturally, and economically diverse inner ring suburbs of Cleveland, Ohio. The combined population numbers approximately 63,000, of which 40 percent are minorities. CHUHPL is a school district library with one main building and three neighborhood branches, all within an eleven-square-mile area. The library's mission is to be "a vital and dynamic community resource that promotes life-long learning."

The staff of 180 includes approximately 60 pages and 27 MLS librarians. Circulation in 2002 was 1.9 million items, or 30.4 items per capita. The library has strong support and backing of the community.

In response to community needs, a separate young adult services department was created in November 2002. A young adult services coordinator was hired to develop this department's collection, outreach, and programming. Job Shadow Day was one of the first successful programs to be implemented by the new department/coordinator.

Young Adult Demographics

Approximately 15 percent of the total service population is between the ages of ten and nineteen. Of the total students enrolled in school, 43 percent attend public schools and 13 percent attend private schools. In addition, a significant number are home-schooled. The public school enrollment is 75 percent African-American, 20 percent Caucasian, 3 percent multiracial, and 2 percent Hispanic and other minorities. The Ohio Department of Education has placed the schools on Academic Watch. The district graduation rate is 78 percent.

Program Participants

Our young adult services department serves eleven- to nineteen-year-olds. The target audience for this program included local public and private high school students as well as home-schooled students.

Thirteen young adults attended this program. There were eight public high school students and five home-

schooled students. Seven students were male and six were female. Nine students were African-American and four were Caucasian.

Youth Participation

Two younger staff members provided input in planning and also participated in the program as staff panelists. Three young adult volunteers recruited heavily among their classmates in order to encourage minority students to attend. Each participant evaluated the program in writing at the conclusion of Job Shadow Day.

Staff and Volunteers

Seventeen staff members representing all library departments and two volunteers were involved in this program as planners or active participants.

Budget

Funded by our Anne Bauer Staff Development Fund, the direct costs for this program were for refreshments and lunch for the young adult attendees and the staff participants. Indirect costs were for salaries/staff time in planning, promoting, hosting, presenting, and evaluating as listed below.

Staff Participants	Hours	Cost
Young adult coordinator	8.0	$160
Training and staff development coordinator	6.0	$120
Human resource coordinator	1.0	$20
Seven panelists (30 minutes each at an average $15/hr)	3.5	$60
Seven department hosts (2 hours each at an average $15/hr)	14.0	$210
Food		$110
Total	**32.5**	**$680**

Evaluation

Job Shadow Day participants evaluated the program in writing. The young adult coordinator and the training and staff development coordinator reviewed the evaluations and prepared a demographic study of the participants. All of the evaluations were extremely positive, and several offered suggestions for future Job Shadow Days. More time for shadowing was requested. The participants also asked for the scope of the program to include special and academic libraries. The next Job Shadow Day is already in the planning stages and will target promotion to community organizations that support young adults, schools (including the Career Prep Advisory Board), the home-school networks, youth development organizations, and the local recreation board.

Impact of the Program

This program is important because it makes a difference in the lives of young adults and addresses many community concerns. Here are the top ten reasons this particular program is important:

1. It sparks the idea that young adults need to prepare for the future, make a plan, investigate their options, and shadow or gain experience to test their ideas about employment against the reality.

2. It promotes the idea of a library career to young adults who may be uncertain about their career choice.

3. It provides an opportunity for young adults to get to know librarians as a step toward community building and mutual understanding.

4. It ties into a new, developing young adult career series at the library that includes résumé writing, interviewing, job skills awareness, a career fair, and librarianship. In addition, it supplements career prep and vocational programs in the local community that focus heavily on technology.

5. It addresses numerous developmental assets from the Forty Development Assets for Adolescents that have been identified by the Search Institute (www.search-institute.org). These include external assets, such as empowerment and boundaries and expectations, and internal assets, such as commitment to learning and positive identity.

6. It addresses library recruitment. A headline in the March 2002 issue of *American Libraries* read, "Numbers reveal need for major recruitment effort." Almost half of our twenty-seven MLS librarians are expected to retire by 2113. It also supports recruitment efforts aimed at minority students. It ties into the library's efforts to focus on pages as a source for future librarians, which is an approach not found in current recruitment literature.

7. It helps build partnerships between local schools, home-school networks, the library, and the School of Library and Information Science at Kent State University.

8. It addresses the City of Cleveland Heights vision (a citizen-driven planning process) "to expose young people to interesting careers, cutting edge technology and innovation, and excellence in the workplace."

9. It opens the door for future partnerships with other community stakeholders.

10. It shows that a medium-sized library can participate successfully in a national ALA initiative—Job Shadow Day.

For More Information

Nancy Levin
Young Adult Coordinator
Cleveland Heights-University Heights Public Library
2345 Lee Rd.
Cleveland Heights, OH 44118
(216) 932-3600, ext. 292
(216) 932-0932 (fax)
nlevin@heightslibrary.org

3. Creative Expression

The programs featured in this section encourage creativity and self-expression in teens as well as promote technical skills in their respective media. The South Shore Video Contest encourages young adults to get involved in the program at whatever level feels comfortable to them, providing a role for teens who prefer to offer background support as well as those who love the limelight. The Zine Project cleverly puts a new spin on the traditional school literary publication, thereby inspiring students to new heights of creativity. Both projects showcase the works of young adults, which reflect their challenges, concerns, and life outlook.

South Shore Video Contest

Duxbury (Mass.) Free Library

Target Audience

Middle, junior high, and senior high school students

Program Description

For three summers running, the young adult department of the Duxbury (Mass.) Free Library (DFL), has hosted a video contest for teens. Open to all teens in the southeastern region of Massachusetts, it has evolved into a truly collaborative effort in which public librarians, teachers, school media specialists, teen youth leaders, and church group leaders have engaged the youth with whom they work to create videotapes.

Original videos produced by individual teens or groups that run no longer (and sometimes much shorter) than twenty minutes can be entered. With a deadline of early August, the contest makes for a nice summer reading activity, but entries from the preceding school year are also accepted. A gala ceremony is held in late August at which awards in many different categories (all group awards, no individual) are given out.

Sponsoring Institution

DFL is the host of the South Shore Video Contest. As one of the few libraries in southeastern Massachusetts to have a young adult librarian, it has the personnel resources to devote to creating the paperwork, organizing the entries, and hosting the judging and the awards ceremony.

The town of Duxbury has a population of 15,000. The library is open 50.8 hours per week, has 12,261 registered borrowers, and is a member of the Old Colony Library Network as well as a member of the South-Eastern Massachusetts Library System. The library is located on the campus of the Duxbury elementary and middle school and across the street from the high school, making it easy to host after-school activities for teens. The public access TV studio is located within the high school building, which makes coordinating editing and shooting opportunities convenient.

Young Adult Demographics

The school population of Duxbury (K–12) is approximately 3,000. Duxbury High School has a population of approximately 800, and Duxbury Middle School (grades seven and eight) has a population of approximately 400. In a survey done by the Duxbury Student Union Initiative, the following statistics were cited: 20 percent of Duxbury students grades seven through ten said they spend most of their time hanging out alone after school. Fifty percent of students, grades seven through ten, spend their after-school time with their friends at the home of a friend. This number increased to 70 percent for grades eleven and twelve.

Program Participants

The participants in the video contest have been teens in grades seven through twelve. They have ranged from individual students who submit videos they did for school assignments, skateboard enthusiasts, and artistic

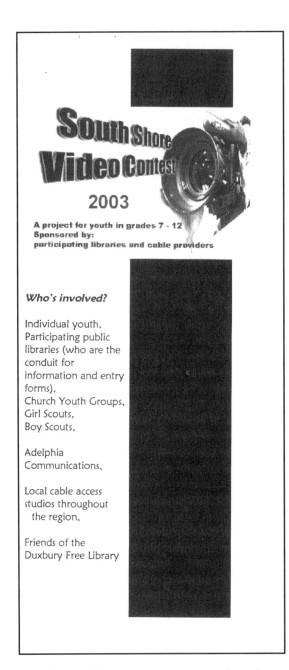

Who's involved?

Individual youth,
Participating public libraries (who are the conduit for information and entry forms),
Church Youth Groups,
Girl Scouts,
Boy Scouts,

Adelphia Communications,

Local cable access studios throughout the region,

Friends of the Duxbury Free Library

Youth Participation

Three youth helpers coordinate the passing out of the awards, musical interludes, and room decoration for the awards ceremony. Otherwise, youth involvement focuses on the entries themselves—planning and executing their projects to artistic satisfaction and to meet contest requirements is a challenging task.

Staff and Volunteers

In 2002, staff included one program coordinator, eleven adult volunteers (including judges), and three teen helpers on awards night.

Budget

Adelphia Cable TV provides licensing fees for use of BMI and ASCAP music.

The Friends of the Duxbury Free Library provide $1,000 to be spent on trophies, refreshments, videotape, paper goods. T-shirts were designed for all the participants that feature the words "Production Crew" on the front and "South Shore Video Contest" on the back with an appropriate logo.

Evaluation

Evaluation input is requested from participants. This is done with a form filled out by participants at the awards ceremony, then a full rehashing and planning of the upcoming event is done at the midwinter meeting by library and school adult leaders. An e-mail list is maintained by the program coordinator, and all previous years' materials are saved electronically. Press coverage is saved physically.

Impact of the Program

The impact of the South Shore Video Contest on participants is varied. Many of the participants enjoy the camaraderie of being part of a group event, one in which they can be a ham in front of the camera or a techie behind it. Oftentimes groups, such as the church group and the teen mentoring group, have members who participated only very tangentially—holding a mike, setting up the filming area, making editorial comments. These kids LOVED being included at a very low-risk, safe comfort level.

Other participants used their considerable imaginations to develop plots and sketch out scenes in which they and their friends acted. Two years ago, one boy wrote original music for his friend's video. He is going on to college to major in music composition, and his friend is heading to film school. One of our winners three years ago entered his South Shore entry in the Nickelodeon After-School Special children's video contest and won the honor of having his video aired on Nickelodeon TV!

types who have elaborate equipment at their fingertips, to church groups documenting a service project and an inner-city peer mentoring group (Brockton Alliance for Youth) who entered two years running with videos they produced from skits they wrote to teach younger kids the pitfalls of careless behavior.

Because the video contest ceremony itself is taped for public access TV, the audience for the South Shore Video Contest becomes greater than merely the active participants. Many teens, children, and adults enjoy watching the public access program that results from the awards ceremony (which included clips from each of the entries), and there is a buzz created in the communities and in the press about the teens, their original ideas, and the library as the sponsoring agent of this unique event.

In 2002, thirty entries represented the work of approximately one hundred teens.

The teens from Brockton, Massachusetts, who have done two films on teen decision-making with regard to sex and drugs have seen their videos featured at local conferences on youth awareness issues. They look back fondly at the time they spent together and are proud of the work that they produced, which can be used over and over again to reach out to other teens.

Other entries included short, clever videos that feature poetry, dance, Spanish, music, clay animation, sports, and crazy reality situations. Younger teens have watched with awe at the more sophisticated efforts of their older counterparts. The impact of the contest has been to empower teens to create a vision, take a risk, and produce a work of art. All this is done in an atmosphere of fun, with a bit of goofing off at awards night, and the understanding that their work is worthy of notice.

For More Information

Ellen Snoeyenbos
Duxbury Free Library
77 Alden St.
Duxbury, MA 02332
(781) 934-2721, ext. 106
(781) 934-0663 (fax)
ellens@ocln.org

The Zine Project

Francis W. Parker School, Chicago

Target Audience

Middle school students

Program Description

The Zine Project was a collaborative effort between an English teacher and a school librarian at the Francis W. Parker School. The two shared an interest in the world of independent writing and publishing. For years the librarian had self-published zines, or independent photocopied mini-magazines of personal writing to be shared with anyone interested. Together the teacher and librarian worked with four sections of sixth graders over a period of three months as they wrote, typed, drew, edited, designed, and marketed their own zines.

Sponsoring Institution

Parker is a private, progressive junior kindergarten through twelfth-grade school in Chicago's Lincoln Park neighborhood. The library serves the entire school. The library staffs two full-time librarians as well as one full-time and two part-time staff members. The school itself is divided into a lower, middle, and upper school within the same building. The librarians have built a solid relationship with the faculty of the middle school. They are a group that is very open to collaboration and new ideas.

Young Adult Demographics

The sixth grade at Parker is comprised of 65 eleven- and twelve-year-olds of Caucasian, African-American, Hispanic, and Asian backgrounds. Parker students are primarily upper-middle class, with approximately 20 percent receiving financial aid.

Program Participants

Sixth grade is the first year of middle school for Parker students. The grade is divided into sections A through D, each with sixteen to eighteen students, and the students remain with those sections as they travel from class to class. In the 2002–2003 school year, the sixth-grade students were an extremely bright, cooperative, and enthusiastic group.

Youth Participation

Each section of sixth-grade students created (and sometimes battled over) a zine title that acted as a theme to help unify a section's worth of writing. Students were assigned jobs as editors, fact-finders, artists, proofreaders, and those who took care of layout. Every student played a role.

The adult supervisors did little to stop the creative flow of each section. Students awed us with their sensitive writing and made us laugh with their absurdity. While students had to be reminded of deadlines, they were never at a loss for ideas. Every article and picture came from the creative minds of sixth-grade students writing about things they enjoyed. The students then decided where each article fit into the zine and what was missing. Very few decisions were made without the students' input.

Staff and Volunteers

This project was a collaborate effort between one school librarian, Julie Halpern-Cordell, and the sixth-grade English teacher, George Drury. During the previous two years at Parker, Halpern-Cordell and Drury had explored their common interests of independent publishing and comic books. Together they had printed a series of poetry broadsides incorporating student writing and drawing. Since Halpern-Cordell had published two different zines of her own over the past seven years, Drury suggested that they attempt a large-scale zine project involving every sixth-grade student.

Budget

Funding was taken from two sources. Drury set aside $10 per student through the English department budget for student publishing fees. The middle school also provides $9 per student for photocopying throughout the school year.

Photocopying in-house proved cheaper (although more time-consuming) than price comparisons with Office Depot and Kinkos.

800 color copies x $.25	$200
9,400 black-and-white copies x $.03	$282
TOTAL	$482

Layout and copying were all done during normal work hours over a period of several weeks.

Evaluation

Evaluation of the Zine Project is ongoing. Next year's students will be more involved in the folding and stapling process (which was done by faculty this year). Proofreading will also be done more cautiously, as we are finding small yet pesky mistakes that students have helped us address with correction fluid and pencils. The production and teamwork were invaluable. The students enjoyed the creative process, which was evi-

dent by their commitment and hard work. The final products speak for themselves as valuable and fulfilling lessons in writing and self-publishing. After the students receive their final copies of the zine, they are asked to write about the zine experience. This form of critical writing stems directly from their journals, which they keep for eight months.

Impact of the Program

Sixth grade at Parker is a very appropriate year to incorporate the Zine Project. Writing is a large part of the curriculum. Poems, journal entries, essays, and response papers are written throughout the year. By the spring, sixth-graders are blossoming into individuals with distinctive voices and ideas. While the faculty recognized the need to provide a level of structure, the results of the Zine Project were completely student-created.

Halpern-Cordell visited Drury's classroom on Thursdays. They began the process in mid-March and scheduled class meetings every other week. The first meeting introduced the students to the world of grassroots publishing. Zines were shared with the students to explain the different content and styles, including poetry, opinion pieces, photocopied photographs, comic strips, clip art, short stories, movie reviews, and fake advertisements. The students were jazzed!

The sections would be producing their own zines over the course of the next two months. Drury had pulled aside some previous class work from each student to ensure that there was a good mix of older and newer pieces. The students contributed fresh work each session.

The zine release party took place on Friday, May 30, 2002, during a lunch period. All sections were present to trade zines and celebrate.

The Zine Project is successful at many levels. The writing skills are heavily curriculum-based, and using them for a pleasant, creative experience allows students to see education work in real-life circumstances. The project increased the students' autonomy as producers of language as they chose themes and concepts and executed the plan in the zines. Because there are many types of writing represented and various jobs that students may perform, this project reaches students of different learning abilities.

Next year, Parker will open its writing and publishing center, and the sixth grade will be ahead of the game by understanding how to work as a team and how to combine genres into a common theme.

The Zine Project has helped the grade to identify themselves as a group that enjoys writing and is open to new ideas about independent publishing. The faculty were highly involved in each student's process, which allowed students to observe collaboration between a teacher and a librarian. The adults acted as a model of teamwork, and students were responsive to this friendship. In turn, the students built trusting relationships with Halpern-Cordell as a librarian. Writing is associated with reading, and the importance of both is emphasized in this program.

For More Information

Julie Halpern-Cordell
George Drury
Francis W. Parker School
300 W. Webster Ave.
Chicago, IL 60614
(773) 353-3000
jhalperncordell@nssd112.org
gdrury@fwparker.org

All of the programs featured in this section are designed to provide teens with information and skills that they will need to survive as adults in today's society. Rather than one-time-only events, each of these programs represents a more comprehensive approach to addressing the needs of young adults through a series of programs, classes, displays, author visits, and collection development strategies. They also involve collaboration between community agencies and youth input to respond to the unique demographics of local teens.

LOVE and SEX: Making Choices

Flint (Mich.) Public Library

Target Audience

Middle, junior high, and senior high school at-risk students

Program Description

The LOVE and SEX: Making Choices program brought together a number of elements that grew out of a community effort to inform teens about the importance of taking charge of their sexual lives and was the founding piece of what was then developed into the Teen-Author Forum.

As a member of Community Matters, a coalition of community youth service providers, young adult librarian Leslie Acevedo engaged in innumerable discussions about the need to create safe spaces for dialogue about sex. When the Genesee Coalition on Adolescent Pregnancy, Parenting, and Prevention (GCAPPP) asked the library to house a national exhibition of photographs and audio stories by photographer Michael Nye around teen pregnancy titled "Children of Children: Portraits of Teenage Parents," library staff saw it as an

Flint Public Library

November/December • 2002   *Vol. 14*

Children of Children; An Exhibit

The Flint Public Library is pleased to house the exhibition "Children of Children-Portraits of Teenage Parents," from November 15 through December 13. The exhibit is a collection of stories of men and women ranging in age from 12 to 100 whose lives have been crucially affected by teenage pregnancy.

This powerful exhibit features 50 black and white photographs accompanied by audio stories told by the individuals in the pictures. In simple and eloquent detail, these narratives draw us closer into each life by addressing many of the complex issues of family, culture, religion, trust, money, education, guilt and responsibility.

This important photographic record is sponsored by the Genesee Coalition on Adolescent Pregnancy, Parenting and Prevention (GCAPPP). Funding for the exhibit is provided by the Ruth Mott Foundation and the Flint Women and Girls Fund of the Community Foundation of Greater Flint.

To extend the conversation about teen pregnancy, the Flint Public Library received a grant from the Community Foundation of Greater Flint to purchase materials for the library collection and organize a community reading event culminating in an author visit. We are inviting individuals and/or groups of girls to read *Like Sisters on the Homefront*, an award winning young adult novel that chronicles the events that follow a 14 year old girl after she becomes pregnant for the second time. The author, Rita Williams-Garcia, plans to visit the library on December 4 when we will all come together to share our thoughts about the novel and the wrenching life changes that come with premature parenthood. Ms. Williams-Garcia's other two YA novels (*Fast Talk on a Slow Track* and *Blue Tights*) both were met with awards and acclaim. Her novels deal with a universality of issues that young adults will find compelling. Copies of *Like Sisters on the Homefront* are available in Browsing Library. For information call 249-2173.

Native American Pottery

Shirley Brauker was born in Angola, Indiana to a Grand Traverse Odawa mother and a German father and grew up naturally integrating the two cultures. Shortly after high school, Shirley married and moved to Michigan where she began raising a family and continuing her education. She received a Bachelors of Fine Arts and a Masters of Fine Arts from Central Michigan University.

She works in various mediums such as pottery and painting and sculpture.

Her trademark is pottery using a decorative "cutout" approach to tell stories of her heritage. She and her husband own Moon Bear Pottery which is " dedicated to the preservation of American Indian art." Her work is authentic in design and legend, and true to the Indian ideal showing great respect for nature and mankind.

Ms. Brauker will visit the library on Saturday, November 9. Her morning presentation is for adults and is a presentation about the nature of her work. In the afternoon she will lead a practical pottery class for children and their families. All materials will be provided. For information call 249-2170.

opportune time to frame conversations around a chosen work of fiction that each teen would read.

The conversation that would arise from the reading would bring teens to the library and would be led by the author herself. Library staff members were aware of how few teens willingly read fiction unless the immediate relevancy is very obvious. The combination of the teen pregnancy exhibit, a trip to the library, and a very candid conversation with the author of a book they just read was designed to spark teens' interest.

Like Sisters on the Homefront by Rita Williams-Garcia was selected as a fiction title that discussed the

LOVE and SEX: Making Choices, Teen-Author Forum Visit
Author: Rita Williams-Garcia
Flint Public Library, 1026 E. Kearsley Street, Flint, Michigan, 48503

Photos: *Children of Children: Portraits of Teen Parents exhibit.* Photos by M. Nye

and a bookmobile. FPL's main library is a central resource in the City of Flint and Genesee County (population 436,141) for research and information, and it is visited everyday by citizens of all ages. The facility is located centrally in Flint's Cultural Center. An ideal focal point for city-wide teen programming, it is also strategically located next to Flint Central High School, Whittier Middle School, and Sarvis-Pierce Elementary School. It is easily accessible via the citywide bus system.

Young Adult Demographics

Flint teens numbered more than 64,800 in the 2000 Census. Nineteen percent live in child poverty (ranking Genesee County 73 of 83 counties in Michigan); 37.1 percent of teens receive free or reduced school lunches. The teen pregnancy rate is 33.2 out of 1,000 (rank 75 out of 81). The high school dropout rate is 4.1 percent (rank 44 out of 80).

Genesee County is a community where child poverty in ages eleven through nineteen has increased by 13 percent, ranking 78 out of 83 counties. Thirty-seven percent more children are receiving free or reduced-price school lunches in 1999 than 1990. Abuse or neglect cases have risen by 204 percent over a ten-year period, and the unemployment rate is 11.6 percent in the City of Flint. Forty-six percent of the total births in Genesee County in 1998 were "non-marital," which ranks 64 out of 70 counties rated in Michigan.

The above figures, taken from the *Kids Count in Michigan 2002 Data Book* (Michigan League for Human Services, 2002), underscore the importance of taking the library programs into the community to reach teens who are in stressful family situations and are not likely to participate in positive reading activities on a regular basis, if at all.

Program Participants

FPL purchased five hundred copies of *Like Sisters on the Homefront* and disseminated all of the copies to middle and high school classes in the Flint-Genesee County community schools.

The two classroom forums were attended by more than 550 students; an evening program for the general public was attended by thirty to forty people. The

issues of teens and teen pregnancy, and the author was invited to lead the book discussions. Multiple copies of the book were made available to teens, classrooms, and community organizations wishing to participate. Teachers and group leaders were also provided with a curriculum guide to support the book. Groups of teens came to the library to meet and discuss the book with the author, tour the photo/audio story exhibit, and take home materials on teen health, pregnancy, and other community resource materials from our community resource table.

The fiction and nonfiction collection was updated with materials on teen pregnancy, sexuality, and body health issues, which were featured in the library's teen area. A bookmark that listed library materials, Internet resources, and local community resources was sent out to all high school classrooms and community health organizations in Flint.

Sponsoring Institution

Serving an urban, underserved, population of 124,943 residents (according to the 2000 Census), Flint Public Library (FPL) is a mid-sized library system in Michigan. It has a centrally located main library, three branches,

exhibit was viewed by more than eight hundred people of all ages.

FPL's LOVE and SEX: Making Choices bookmark was sent out to all county middle and high schools and community health centers and teen organizations, as well as offered to library patrons. More than twelve thousand bookmarks have been disseminated to date.

Library materials, both fiction and nonfiction, on topics of teen parenting, human reproduction, and sexual health topics were updated and expanded. Ninety-two books, videos, audiotapes, and DVDs were added to this collection, and these items circulated more than 467 times from September 2002 to March 2003.

Youth Participation

Youth input was sought on the selection of materials for the resource collection; teens also reviewed books as they were received before they were added to the collections. Young adults also were the main source for evaluating the success of the programs, and their feedback was sought at every opportunity and was the basis of the library's report back to our outside funders—GCAPPP.

Testimonials

Testimonials were taken from teens and teachers who attended the Teen-Author Forum with author Rita Williams-Garcia. Their comments included the following:

"I opened the book and read that first page and said, 'This book is about me.'"

"My students are reading . . . and enjoying the book without me having to nag them."

"I love her books and now want to read all her books."

"It was so cool to talk to the author who wrote the book you just read and loved. . . . It was like I could have a personal conversation with her about the parts I loved, the parts I hated or did not think were right . . . or I could learn the true story behind the story. She was so nice . . ."

"This was a marvelous forum. My students were reading every day and wanted to discuss the book together. Then they wanted to get copies of [Williams-Garcia's] other books. This was so meaningful for them. And then having this exhibit here at the same time . . . just wonderful!"

"The combination of the exhibit and the literature was a total classroom packet. It also came at the time we were examining fiction versus nonfiction literature in our classroom . . . so this was great! . . . and the students loved the book."

"This would be great if we could do this again next year. If we knew ahead of time we could plan to come more than once. It was very interesting to have so many classrooms from different schools reading and talking about the same book at the same time. Meeting the author was very exciting for my students. Many of them love writing and enjoyed hearing stories of how Rita Williams-Garcia became a writer and her career as a writer."

"I love the book. I know so many kids who have the same story that Gayle did."

"I read the book and said, 'This is my story.' I too, am pregnant for the second time and yet I want to make something of my life too. It is so hard."

Staff and Volunteers

There were two library staff members involved in the planning and implementation of the programs: the young adult librarian and the supervisor of services to children and young adults.

Budget

This program was funded through three sources: FPL; a grant written by the library staff to the Community Foundation of Greater Flint—Women and Young Girls Fund; and GCAPPP.

Flint Public Library:

Two staff librarians ($25/hr x 30 hrs)	$ 750
Author honorarium for book discussion, meals, hotel, and travel expenses (three meetings)	$2,100
Total	**$2,850**

Community Foundation of Greater Flint, Women and Young Girls Fund 2002–2003

Collection resources (books, videos, and audiotapes)	$1,500
Bibliographies/bookmarks (15,000)	$1,000
Total	**$2,500**

Genesee Coalition on Adolescent Pregnancy, Parenting, and Prevention

Exhibit "Children Having Children: Stories of Teen Parents" Exhibit cost and community publicity	no cost estimates available

Evaluation

The additional ninety-two books, videos, audiotapes, and DVDs that were added to the young adult collection have circulated more than 467 times since September 2002.

Surveys were collected after programs from both teens and teachers. Individuals were asked to fill out a response form after viewing the exhibit "Children of Children."

Impact of the Program

Fiction holds a special place in the lives of all readers. It is between the pages of books that many young people first ride a horse, travel to a foreign country, learn about the emotion of death and grief, learn what first love is about, or come to understand that in some situations making the right or wrong decisions will have a lasting effect on the rest of our lives. It is through trying on emotions and decisions at the expense of the book's characters that readers learn from or think about the larger message the author hopes to convey. Teen literature is especially strong in raising important issues for

teens at the time in their lives where emotions, decisions, and the quest for answers run with urgency.

The guided reading experience and author visit, combined with the expanded selection of library materials and Michael Nye's photo/audio story exhibit, "Children of Children" (locally sponsored by GACPPP), presented a powerful package for teens to experience. Many young adults were moved by this program.

For More Information

Leslie A. Acevedo
Young Adult Services Librarian
Flint Public Library
1026 E. Kearsley St.
Flint, MI 48502
(810) 232-7111
(810) 249-2633 (fax)
lacevedo@flint.lib.mi.us

Teen Empowerment Project

Queens Borough Public Library, Jamaica, N.Y.

Target Audience

At-risk high school students

Program Description

The Teen Empowerment Project is a program that uses early intervention to help prevent the possible escalation of violence perpetrated by young adults. In partnership with the Queens district attorney's office, the program directs youth ages sixteen through nineteen and first-time, nonviolent offenders toward improving academic performance and preparing for post-secondary school success and the workforce. The district attorney's office refers these teens to the library twice a year for a twelve-week program. The objective is to empower the teens, aid them in becoming productive members of society, and encourage them to be lifelong library users. Towards this goal, the program offers these teens career counseling, self-esteem and health workshops, computer training, armed forces and college recruiting, and other resources that will enable them to make positive and productive decisions.

Sponsoring Institution

Founded in 1896, Queens Borough Public Library (QBPL) serves the Queens population of 2.2 million—the most ethnically diverse county in the nation. The library has sixty-three library facilities—one within walking distance of every Queens resident. QBPL circulates more books

and other materials than any other library system in the United States. It has the highest per capita usage rate of the three independent New York City public library systems. During fiscal year 2002, the library reported that it:

- served 16.3 million customers;

- circulated 16.8 million items;

- received 1.25 million hits on its Web site each month;

- provided more than 24,000 free programs;

- answered 4.69 million reference and directional inquiries; and

- presented more than 20,000 programs for more than 500,000 people.

Young Adult Demographics

According to the 2000 census, there are more than 210,000 people ages twelve through nineteen living in Queens County. In Queens, those teens attend more than seventy middle, junior high, and high schools. Many of the schools are overcrowded. They are also in need of extra services because 40 percent of people in Queens were born outside of the United States, are from more than 100 countries, and speak more than 140 languages. New York City, like many other large urban areas, has many at-risk factors that affect the lives of teens in Queens County. They include:

- 8,571 children are homeless;

- every 4 days, a young person under nineteen is murdered;

- more than 50 percent of students read below grade level;

- every week, 16,080 young people use mental health services;

- every day, 147 young people are reported abused or neglected;

- 9 percent of teens have carried weapons to school;

- 16 out of 1,000 teens are in foster care;

- 50.4 percent of children in NYC are born into poor families;

- 20.0 percent of teens receive some form of public assistance;

- 9.6 percent of all live births are to teen mothers; and

- 8 percent of all youth attempt suicide (girls, 11 percent; boys, 5 percent).

Program Participants

For three and a half hours each week for a twelve-week period, ten to fifteen teens ages sixteen to nineteen participate in the QBPL's Teen Empowerment Project. These teens are referred to the library from the Queens district attorney's office, where they are involved in the Second Chance program. The Second Chance program is composed of young people who have pleaded guilty to low-level misdemeanors. During the Second Chance program, young people do community service, such as cleaning parks and scraping graffiti off of walls. In exchange for successfully completing the program, the district attorney's office recommends to the judge to dismiss all charges and seal their records.

In 1999, QBPL proposed a program to Queens district attorney Richard Brown. Rather than administer punishment detail and other community service, the library would offer an alternative to teens in the Second Chance program, with the goal of modifying negative behavior patterns, increasing the use of library resources, and empowering the teens to take charge of their lives. The district attorney's office agreed to refer fifteen teens for a pilot eight-week program to receive career counseling, computer classes, and a graduation ceremony. Since then, the program has expanded to twelve weeks to include more programming.

From December 1999 to April 2003, ten sessions of this program were completed. In the first 10 rounds, 133 teens have finished the program.

Youth Participation

During the last workshop before graduation, the teens are given an survey that asks them to evaluate all the workshops they experienced during the twelve-week period. The feedback is invaluable and used to design the program that will be presented to the next group. Each of the ten rounds completed has been slightly different based on the feedback of the teens.

Staff and Volunteers

This program has been an internal collaboration between young adult services and the library's investigation and security department. A staff member from the security department is the link between the library, the district attorney's office, and the New York Police Department (NYPD). A staff member from YA services sets up the twelve-week schedule, contacts speakers, sends out contracts, books room locations, and is in charge of overall coordination and supervision of the program. Two employees from the program and services department provide supervision during the actual workshop. The library's webmaster from the information and technology department teaches computer skills two hours a week.

Budget

Initially the funding for this program was provided exclusively through the city budget for young adult library services. In late 2002, the library received a small grant from New York State to conduct this program. The current budget is as follows:

Cost components

Two career counseling workshops	$250
Two self-esteem workshops	$600
One talk with two felons	$200
Refreshments for graduation	$ 60
Total per twelve-week program	$1,110

Non-cost components

NYPD understanding workshop (four NYPD officers attend for one and a half hours)
Armed Forces recruitment (two members of the Armed Forces attend for one hour)
Health workshop (one person from local hospital attends for one hour)
College workshop (one person from local college attends for one hour)

In-kind components

Library awareness workshop (conducted by coordinator of YA services for one and a half hours)
Career Zone online workshop (conducted by coordinator of YA services for one and a half hours)
Computer training (conducted by Queens Library webmaster for twenty hours)

Staff time

YA coordinator: 25 hours @ $ 29.90 per hour
Coordinates and supervises program, and presents two sessions.
Assistant coordinator: 8 hours @ $ 24.88 per hour
Supervises three programs.
Assistant director of programs and services: 8 hours @ $ 34.02 per hour
Supervises three programs.
Assistant director of investigations and security: 20 hours @ $ 34.02 per hour
Coordinates communications with district attorney's office and NYPD, and supervises three programs.
Webmaster, from information and technology: 20 hours @ $ 29.57 per hour

Evaluation

As previously stated, an evaluation is conducted with the teens to see what programs affected them the most and which ones they feel should be expanded or eliminated. The Queens district attorney's office has also provided verbal feedback. They maintain contact with each teen's family after the program is completed, and they encourage positive corrective behavior within the family. Gail Giordano, assistant district attorney for Queens County and Second Chance coordinator, said there was a "noticeable change from angry kids to kids willing to accept responsibility for their actions." She also informed QBPL that the recidivism rate for the young people that graduate from the library component of the Second Chance program is lower then those that participate in the traditional Second Chance program without the library. The library's program is making a major difference in the lives of these young people.

Impact of the Program

The Teen Empowerment Project is designed to change negative behavior into positive behavior patterns, using library resources to positively channel young adults. The program is directed to teens at risk, ages sixteen to nineteen, helping them develop skills to become productive members of a complex, technological society. The program offers skills development so they are better able to take control of how they live their lives. During the twelve weeks the participants gain insight into the options available to every teen after graduation from high school: college, armed forces, employment, and jail—which is not an option at all. These options, and other important information, such as health and self-esteem, are presented during the following workshops:

■ Library awareness—teens get library card cleared of fines and tour of resources in the Central Library.

- Understanding workshop—NYPD sends community officers to speak to the teens and listen to their concerns and answer their questions.

- Felon talk—two men in their twenties speak to the group about their experiences in prison and how a felony record follows them after they serve their time.

- Health talk—local hospital representatives speak to the group about various health topics.

- Self-esteem workshop—a member of New York Youth-At-Risk speaks to the group about were they are and where they envision themselves in five years.

- Career counseling—the group learns résumé writing, interview techniques, and job-finding strategies.

- Career Zone training—online training on the New York State Department of Labor's interactive Web site for teens.

- Armed Forces talk—a local recruiter provides information about opportunities in the Armed Forces.

- College talk—a local college provides information about college and its importance in finding more opportunities in the workforce.

- Computer training—a library volunteer teaches many of the Microsoft Office programs and shows how these tools can be useful when looking for employment or going to school.

- Graduation—celebration and recognition of teens who completed the program.

At each graduation ceremony, one of the participants speaks about his or her experience during the program. At the graduation in February 2000, Rebecca Hillman expressed her thoughts: "We're not proud of the way we got here, but it's good to know that we received a second chance. This program has educated us on things we need to know throughout life. We've had a chance to meet new, exciting, and interesting people. People taught us things we didn't know, and helped us with things we didn't understand." In January 2002, Nikina Matthews stated, "This program is such a big influence on young people like myself. I would refer anybody to the program, and I just wanted to thank the Second Chance program for letting me get the opportunity to attend these sessions."

For More Information

Nick Buron
89-11 Merrick Blvd.
Jamaica, NY 11432
(718) 990-8545
(718) 291-8936 (fax)
NBuron@queenslibrary.org

Think Green! Find Your Fortune

The Wadsworth (Ohio) Public Library

Target Audience

Middle school, junior high, and senior high school students

Program Description

The Think Green! Find Your Fortune campaign is focused on promoting financial literacy to young adults. With the right tools, teens can live on their own, finance their own educations, start businesses doing what they love to do, and invest in the stock market. The Think Green campaign is striving to teach these tools by establishing and maintaining a financial resource center at the Wadsworth (Ohio) Public Library (WPL) full of resources pertaining to personal money management, investing, and entrepreneurship. While these resources are readily available to those teens already interested in the subject, a series of programs and a marketing campaign was developed in order to reach reluctant young adults. By partnering with various businesses in the area as well as the local high school's marketing students, several programs have been implemented, and one more is planned for the future.

Sponsoring Institution

WPL is an independent library serving the citizens of the Wadsworth area, city and township. Wadsworth is a semi-rural Ohio town with a population of about 19,000 people. This middle-class community is located in Medina County, about fifteen miles west of Akron and forty miles south of Cleveland off of Interstate 76.

The library has a young adult services department and one young adult services librarian who develops and maintains the teen collection, plans programming, and supervises an active teen advisory board. An intermediate school, a middle school, and a high school are all located within walking distance of the library and have total enrollments of 2,724 students. There is also one parochial school for grades K–8 nearby.

Young Adult Demographics

There are approximately 2,800 teens enrolled at schools served by WPL. The population is largely Caucasian; only one percent of the teens are Asian. According to the *MDR Ohio School Directory* (Market Data Retrieval, 2002), four percent of Wadsworth's young adults lived at or below the poverty level during the 2002–2003 school year. These students would particularly benefit from the Think Green program.

Program Participants

Young adults ages twelve to eighteen are the intended audience for the Think Green campaign. However, for certain programs, a more specific audience is targeted. For instance, the Real World workshop would be most pertinent to high school seniors, as they are about to graduate and either enter college or the workforce. In addition, special attention is being paid to at-risk teens who attend night school because of failing grades or employment at full-time jobs that are necessary to help support their families.

A total of 896 young adults have attended the three Think Green programs so far. It is difficult to track how many teens have used the financial literacy collection of materials and resources; however, the collection is heavily used and circulates often.

Youth Participation

Members of the Wadsworth High School marketing class were extremely instrumental in getting the Think Green campaign off to a good start. They devised and implemented a survey in order to learn which direction the campaign should head, they developed the slogan and promotional materials, and they helped disseminate information about the programs. Three high school students implemented a marketing plan for the program.

Staff and Volunteers

One staff person is solely responsible for administering the Think Green campaign. A team of five community volunteers from area businesses helped get the campaign off the ground.

Budget

The project has been funded solely through a grant administered by the Ohio Library Foundation called the Drew Carey Grant for Young Adult Services in Ohio. The grant was a gift to Ohio's libraries from Carey after he won $500,000 on *Who Wants to Be a Millionaire?* WPL applied for a portion of this money, and they received $21,000 in June 2001. To date, this money has funded the purchase of a special collection of books and magazines on financial literacy, computer software, and marketing materials, such as custom-made fortune cookies with the slogan, "Find Your Fortune" advertising a collection of Web resources on our Web site. In addition, the money has paid for Checks and Balances, a workshop that taught young adults how to manage a checking account; Take Stock, an interactive game about investing in the stock market; and, most notably, a visit from the Motley Fools, brothers David and Tom

Gardner and the authors of several books, including *The Motley Fool Investment Guide for Teens: Eight Steps to Having More Money than Your Parents Ever Dreamed Of* (Fireside, 2002). Every student at an assembly of high school juniors and seniors received a complementary copy of this book, listened to the Motley Fools' presentation about the importance of saving and investments, then had the opportunity to have their book signed.

Evaluation

It was difficult to evaluate the success of the assembly-sized programs because the students' attendance was mandatory and they were held during school hours. Take Stock, however, was a smaller program, and the young adults in attendance were there voluntarily. This program was evaluated with a form titled "Give Us Your Two Cents." Five simple questions on the form gathered young adults' opinions in terms of how much they learned, how much they enjoyed it, what they liked least, and what they liked best about the programs. Since this was a new series of programs, comparative figures are not available; however, of the young adults who attended the Take Stock program, *all* of them indicated that they would attend similar programs in the future. This fall, the Think Green series of financial literacy programs will wrap up with a program called the Real World, during which teens will pick a profession, be given play money to represent a paycheck, and be asked to rent an apartment, pay taxes, secure auto insurance, and various other activities to demonstrate how much money it takes to live on one's own. A visit from Sharon Flake, author of *Money Hungry* (Jump Sun, 2003) and *Begging for Change* (Jump Sun, 2003) is also in the planning stages to coincide with the Real World program. Every student who attends the program will receive complementary copies of her books.

Impact of the Program

The Think Green campaign is both relevant and important to area teens. While economics and finance are subjects taught in the Wadsworth city schools, students often fail to apply the concepts of saving and investing to their own lives. Many young adults are employed throughout the school year, and even more work during summer vacations, but few use the money they earn for anything other than their own immediate entertainment. Furthermore, a survey we conducted at the outset of this campaign revealed that most young adults do not have checking accounts or credit cards, making the transition from high school to college one fraught with overspending and credit card debt. The Think Green campaign introduces teens to checking accounts and credit cards, as well as to the benefits of compound interest, so that they can practice money management skills while still living at home. With the proper tools, and by understanding the relevance of such topics to their own lives at an earlier age, teens can avoid the hazards of poor money management and grow to become financially successful adults.

For More Information

Valerie A. Ott
Teen Services Librarian
Wadsworth Public Library
132 Broad St.
Wadsworth, OH 44281
(330) 334-5761, ext. 260
(330) 334-6605 (fax)
Valerie.ott@wadsworth.lib.oh.us

Wired for Youth

Austin (Tex.) Public Library

Target Audience

Middle school, junior high, and senior high low-income students

Program Description

The Wired for Youth program provides computer access and literary experiences for children ages eight to eighteen in ten Austin public libraries. The program targets communities where young people are less likely to have adequate computer access at home. Centers have from seven to twelve computers (eighty-two total), and classes and services offered are based on the needs of the youth. Each center has a great deal of autonomy in tailoring activities to local interests. The goal is to provide opportunities for youth to work on homework, participate in computer classes, and enjoy independent time on the computers. Specific classes and events include poetry writing, cultural celebrations, and interest group gatherings. There is a strong focus on reading, writing, and literacy and on youth involvement. Although the primary focus is computers, Wired for Youth provides youth with a holistic learning environment and encourages cooperative learning.

Sponsoring Institution

Austin Public Library (APL) is an urban library system with twenty branches, a central library, and a history center. A department of city government, the library's current budget is $18.8 million, with 325.4 FTE staff members. The youth services division has a staff of 26.5 FTE, with seven Wired for Youth librarians dedicating 100 percent of their time to the Wired for Youth program. Summer interns, called Cyberlifeguards, provide additional staffing. The library has more than 400,000 registered cardholders and circulates more than 3 million items each year. The library is the largest in the central Texas area, and it serves youth without regard to residency. It won the SLJ/Gale Giant Steps Award for its Star Card initiative in 2000. Wired for Youth centers were awarded a "Best of Austin" accolade by the *Austin Chronicle* in 2001, and *Library Journal* named Wired for Youth staff member Michele Gorman a "Mover and Shaker" for 2003.

Young Adult Demographics

Demographics vary somewhat from center to center, but all serve communities that are near or above 50 percent minority population (Hispanic or African-American). While the median household income for Austin is $42,258 per year, most youth served by Wired for Youth centers are in families with significantly lower income. Many local families have limited English-language skills.

Program Participants

Wired for Youth centers serve youth ages eight to eighteen who live in areas of the community where technology is less available at home and in schools.

By the end of the fiscal year (September 2003), the computers in Wired for Youth centers were used for 100,000 sessions. Approximately ten thousand young people attended technology-related programs, classes, and events in 2003. During the previous fiscal year, young adults used computers 77,444 times, and 7,127 attended programs and classes. Since the program began in May 2000, young adults have used the computers more than 200,000 times. Computer sessions can vary from thirty minutes to several hours. Seventy percent of the young people visit the centers at least once a week, and 10 percent are first-time visitors.

Youth Participation

Youth advisory committees help the Wired for Youth librarian determine topics for workshops, programs, classes, and events to be held. A logo contest was held to allow youth to design the Wired for Youth logo, and staff field-tested the Web site to ensure that youth interests were covered, the colors were youth-friendly, and the format followed their thought processes. A Wired Works section of the site allows youth to see their work displayed (internally we refer to this section as the "virtual refrigerator door," as it is used to showcase students' art and writing). Youth also participate in making decisions about the selection of materials (using catalogs to assist in selecting graphic novels and high-interest materials), have spearheaded their own fundraisers to purchase headphones and other items for

Budget

A $500,000 challenge grant from the Michael and Susan Dell Foundation allowed APL to purchase computers, software, and other technology to establish ten Wired for Youth centers in 2000; the grant also provides $42,000 each year for programming, supplies, training, and travel from 2003 to 2005. The tenth center opened in November 2001.

The City of Austin funds full-time youth librarians to manage each center, and the Austin Public Library Foundation (APLF) raises additional funds to enhance the library's youth materials collections and to provide temporary staff support during the summers.

FY 2002–2003 budget	City funds	Austin Public Library Foundation
Staff and benefits	$354,284	$38,250
Supplies	$14,549	$10,000
Mileage/travel for staff	$3,960	$1,000
Printing/advertising	$2,000	$4,000
Speakers/presenters	$5,000	$12,000
Materials for collection	$10,000	$ 5,000
Training for staff		$4,000
Food for programs		$500
Total	**$389,793**	**$74,750**

APLF raised the required $500,000 match for the APL youth collections. APLF also receives funds from Dell Foundation and SBC to fund summer Cyber-lifeguards, paying salaries for library school interns to work part-time in the centers. Since the program's inception, we have also received grants from Noggin for additional software, Webber Family Foundation for class presenters and technology materials for the collection, and Book Boosters to provide temporary staff to cover vacancies. We also receive some in-kind gifts from community groups, such as paper, diskettes, art supplies.

Evaluation

As part of the original grant, the library surveyed users to determine how often they visited the Wired for Youth center, the purpose of their computer use, other computer access available to them, and how they learned about the centers. We also asked whether the respondent had a library card. As might be expected, almost 50 percent of the respondents indicated that they had access to school computers, but 70 percent indicated that they visit the centers at least once a week. Only 30 percent had computers at home.

Monthly statistics are collected to record the number of youth who use the computer centers and attend programs, but we also calculate the percent of available time that the computers are actually used. For the current year, youth are using the computers more than 80 per-

the centers (and then conducted research and voted on the products to purchase), and are involved in writing reviews and articles for the center newsletters. Currently, youth are creating a video advertisement for Wired for Youth. The fierce loyalty to the Wired for Youth centers expressed by the students and their parents is a clear demonstration of the impact the program has had on the lives of Austin's youth.

Staff and Volunteers

Each center is managed by a full-time professional Wired for Youth librarian. Ten Cyberlifeguard interns (library school students) work twenty to thirty hours a week for eight to ten weeks during the summer to provide additional staffing and keep the centers open longer hours. Thanks to additional funding from the Community Foundation received in October 2003, two additional Cyberlifeguard interns have also been working in the centers for fifteen to twenty hours per week during the school year. Volunteers assist on Sundays, during vacations, and other times when additional staffing is needed. The youth services manager manages the program. Total full-time staff is currently 7 FTE, 5 additional FTE for summer and vacations, and 1.75 FTE volunteers. The youth services manager devotes approximately 20 percent of her time to Wired for Youth.

cent of the hours they are available. At some centers, the computers are in use as much as 97 percent of the time.

Since the Wired for Youth program began, annual use has doubled each year. Additional computers have been added to meet demand. Anecdotal reports and personal observation indicate that quiet branches that were not frequented by youth prior to the opening of a Wired for Youth center are now primary destinations for youth. A community member nominated the Wired for Youth program for a Noggin TV grant because he saw firsthand what the Wired for Youth center was accomplishing for kids; we received $2,500 from this grant for additional software and supplies.

Two outside organizations have studied and evaluated the program. According to the University of Texas' LBJ School, "The Wired for Youth program gives children the skills needed to thrive in a technology-saturated world. Most importantly, Wired for Youth provides kids with a safe, secure environment to work on homework, experiment on the computer, and enjoy the support of dedicated staff members who serve as librarians, youth advocates, role models, and friends all in one."

The University of Michigan conducted an outcomes-based evaluation of the Wired for Youth project in 2002. Their report concludes, "We cannot overemphasize the positive outcomes resulting from the interactions between the staff and the participants." It is available at www.si.umich.edu/libhelp/toolkit/AustinReport.html.

Impact of the Program

Kids who never before set foot in the library now come because of the Wired for Youth program. We see the impact through the number of kids who register for library cards because they want to check out a graphic novel after attending a Japanese anime movie program and learning how to use animation software. We see the impact through the sheer numbers of kids (an average of seven thousand per month) who use the computers in the centers. We see the impact every time a child is proud that she can teach another kid what she has learned. Although kids often come into the center for the first time just to play games, chat on the Internet, and hang out with friends, a majority of them return to do homework or to get help from the librarian. Most of the kids are not devoted readers, but they now pick up a book to write a review for the center newsletter or read

poetry to add to a Web site. They proudly bring their parents to the library to see the work they have done, and they often bring their friends in to meet the Wired for Youth librarian. They use their newly developed computer skills to teach their siblings, friends, and parents.

In addition to the standard Microsoft Office suite of software, center computers have animation software, Audacity music software, Photoshop, Swish, and Fireworks, as well as such Web design software as Dreamweaver and Homesite. Young adults are able to obtain one-on-one help, participate in classes, or experiment on their home. Opportunities have included developing a computer game with noted animator Alan Watts (try it out www.datax.com/aquakid), learning to edit digital files, discovering ways to create multimedia projects (see samples of work at www.auntlee.com/museum), and more. A project with the local PBS station on community history and oral biography resulted in family stories that are now a major component of the local PBS Web site for the Tweens program (www.klru.org/tweens/family/index.html).

For More Information

Jeanette Larson
Youth Services Manager
Austin Public Library
P.O. Box 2287
Austin, TX 78768
(512) 974-7405
(512) 974-7403 (fax)
jeanette.larson@ci.austin.tx.us

Wired for Youth Programs   Summer 2003

SUMMER FUN@WFY

June-July: Summer Reading get a clue...READ!
Celebrate summer fun at a Wired for Youth Center in your neighborhood. Weekly special events, summer reading lists, classes, and much more are scheduled throughout the summer. Activities will vary by WFY Center; check the WFY Web site for more information.

Available on wiredforyouth.com: Webliographies on spies, detectives, and mysteries available online to help you select a book to read for the Summer Reading Club. Cool prizes awarded for top book reviews.

Wired@Carver! Youth Advisory Committee——special events
Book Review—like to read? Review books a month before they are available in the bookstore or at the local library.

The Michael & Susan Dell Wired for Youth Centers offer youth from ages 8 to 18 the opportunity to expand their knowledge of computers and the World Wide Web through classes and individual instruction. All Centers have at least seven computers with word processing, graphic design, web design, and animation software, as well as Internet access. The Centers have extended hours for the summer months. Contact the Wired for Youth librarian or check out the WFY Web page at www.wiredforyouth.com for more information about activities at each center.

One-on-one homework help
Free printing for summer school work
Special programs
800 Guadalupe
974-7400

Computer or craft classes most Wednesdays at 3:00 p.m.
Introductory classes on Mondays at 3:00 p.m.
One-on-one instruction available
Free printing for summer school work
Margaret Burnett, Wired for Youth Librarian
651 N. Pleasant Valley Rd.
974-7559
margaret.burnett@ci.austin.tx.us

Weekly contests all summer long!
Computer Classes most Thursdays
One-on-one instruction available
Free printing for summer school work
Patti Cook, Wired for Youth Librarian
5500 Manchaca Road
447-6652
patti.cook@ci.austin.tx.us

Computer classes and special activities
One-on-one instruction
Free printing for summer school home work
Girl Group, for girls ages 10 and up
Weekly contests with prizes
Arts and crafts projects
Martha Dollar, Wired for Youth Librarian
3101 Oak Springs Drive
927-2188
martha.dollar@ci.austin.tx.us

Weekly contests all summer long
Homework help for summer school

Beth Solomon, Wired for Youth Librarian
5803 Nuckols Crossing Road
462-1452
beth.solomon@ci.austin.tx.us

Extra computer time and free printing for summer school homework
Special crafts throughout the summer
Learn how to make cards, flyers, puzzles, and other cool stuff on the computer
Pat Chow, Wired for Youth Librarian
4721 Loyola Lane
926-4684
pat.chow@ci.austin.tx.us

One-on-one homework help
Free printing for summer school work
Special programs
Joanna Nigrelli, Wired for Youth Librarian
5833 Westminster Drive
928-0333
joanna.nigrelli@ci.austin.tx.us

5. Literary Appreciation

In both of the programs featured in this chapter, literature is used as a springboard to introduce students to a variety of related issues. Langston Hughes: A Season on Staten Island relies on a collaboration between a number of community agencies to expose students to different aspects of the life of this renowned poet, incorporating historical information with hands-on farming and visits from guest authors to engage students' interest. Poetry Alive combines a traditional poetry reading with music, art, performance, publications, and author visits to excite students about this art form. Both of these programs are made possible with modest, in-house funding.

Langston Hughes: A Season on Staten Island

The New York Public Library, Staten Island, N.Y.

Target Audience

Middle school students

Program Description

This program introduced intermediate school students on Staten Island to the life and works of Langston Hughes. The program is centered on the summer Hughes worked as a farmhand on Staten Island. The New York Public Library (NYPL) Connecting Libraries and Schools program (CLASP) arranged with the Staten Island Historical Society to let program participants use their farm to grow crops and get a sense of what Hughes experienced. NYPL, the Staten Island Historical Society, and participating teachers developed original materials to be used in the classroom. Two sessions were held at the library with two noted writers and a storyteller—David St. John Mills, Tony Medina, and Joyce Parr—talking about Hughes. After each visit to

the library, students proceeded to the farm, first for planting and later for harvesting. Crops were donated to a local food bank. The story of Hughes on Staten Island is scheduled to be published in the next issue of *The Staten Island Historian*.

Sponsoring Institutions

CLASP is a library-school partnership that links schools serving students in kindergarten through twelfth grade and the three New York City public library systems. In 2002–2003, CLASP programs sponsored by NYPL were attended by 144,835 students. Initiated in 1991 as a national pilot program with private funding, CLASP is a unique collaboration between libraries and schools that brings together teachers, school and public librarians, and parents. CLASP librarians visit local schools to sign up children and parents for library cards, reach out to teachers and school librarians, excite students about good books, and provide workshops for parents to promote reading at home.

The basic program of CLASP services includes:

- library cards for all children in public and private schools;
- class visits in the schools and in the libraries;
- parent workshops that encourage involvement in student education;
- teacher workshops and improved channels of communication for educators;
- family literacy programs to highlight the enjoyment of reading; and
- summer reading booklists and library activities.

Historic Richmond Town is New York City's living history village and museum complex. Visitors can explore the diversity of the American experience, especially that of Staten Island and its neighboring communities, from the colonial period to the present.

Langston Hughes
A Season on Staten Island

THE BIG SEA
Introduction by Arnold Rampersad
LANGSTON HUGHES

BLACK HERITAGE
Langston Hughes

A collaborative project of:

The New York Public Library

HISTORIC RICHMOND TOWN

The NYC Dept. of Education
District 31

Poetry Alive 2003 Schedule
April 4, 2003
Below are listed the classes scheduled to attend. Additional individual passes are available through the library for all periods except 2nd & 3rd. Passes must be

Period 1	Period 2	Period 3	Period 4	Period 5	Period 6
Students	Madrigals & Students	Students & Community	Community & Students	Students	Students
Sanders—7 poets (31)	Sanders—8 poets (31)	Sanders- 3 poets (16)	Sanders-0 poets (20)	Gailey 1-2 poets (10)	McCreary 0 poets (9)
Rickmers 0 poets (35)	Rickmers 0 poets (35)	Rickmers 0 poets (35)	Rickmers 0 poets (35)	McCreary 0 poets (6)	Rickmers 0 poets (35)
Miller – 3poets (35)	Miller 5 poets (35)	Miller 1 poet (35)	Miller 1-2 poets (35)	Ward (35)	Ward (35)
	Marshall 5 poets (35)	Marshall 5 poets (35)	Vetrano	Gulbrandsen 0 poets (31)	Vetrano
McCreary 0 poets (7)	Delgado (7 poets)	Brown (10) & McCreary 0 poets (7)	Lauten ? poets (35)	Lauten ? poets (18) Vetrano	Lauten ? poets (20)
Besnard 9 poets (35)	Besnard 7 poets (35)	Besnard 7 poets (20)	Besnard 9 poets (20)	Sherer (28)	Besnard 8 poets (20)
Gulbrandsen (12)	Sands 6 poets (20)	Morrissey (35)	Morrissey (35)	Morrissey (35)	Sands 7 poets (20)
Total 155	Total 198	Total 193	Total 180	Total 165	Total 139
Readers 18	Readers 28	Readers 20	Readers 20	Readers 3	Readers 15

The village area occupies tweinty-five acres of a hundred-acre site and has about fifteen restored buildings, including homes and commercial and civic buildings, as well as a museum.

Established in 1958, Historic Richmond Town is a joint project of the Staten Island Historical Society, an independent nonprofit cultural organization, and the City of New York, which owns the land and buildings and supports part of its operations with public funds from the Department of Cultural Affairs. The Staten Island Historical Society also receives support from the New York State Department of Education, the New York State Council on the Arts, the Institute of Museum Services, the Office of the Borough President, and private contributions from corporations, foundations, and individuals.

The Staten Island Historical Society operates the elven-acre Decker Farm at 435 Richmond Hill Road, which features a farmhouse, three barns, and four sheds. In addition to the farm's fields the society also raises chickens. It is located within a mile of the original farm where Langston Hughes worked. The Decker Farm sponsors two collaborative farm projects: Council on the Environment of New York City's greenmarket initiative and Cornell University's farmer training project. During the past two years, nearly seven thousand school children from schools in Staten Island, Brooklyn, and Queens participated in pumpkin picking at the farm. The society has also has set aside a portion of the farm to provide the Greenbelt Native Plant Center with a plant nursery.

Young Adult Demographics

The Staten Island schools serve a mix of socio-economic groups. Intermediate School (IS) 49 serves the poorest students on the island. IS 61 serves a mix of lower- and middle-income students, and IS 2 serves primarily middle-income students. Students at these schools, like most other New York City schools, have a wide range of ethnic backgrounds. (See table 1.)

Program Participants

The program introduced seventy-five students in the seventh and eighth grades from IS 2 (The George Egbert School), IS 49 (the Berta A. Dreyfus School), and IS 61 (the William Morris School) on Staten Island. IS 49 and 61 are located on Staten Island's more urban north shore, and IS 2 is located in the more suburban mid-island region. Social studies and language arts classes were selected to participate.

Youth Participation

Students were introduced to Langston Hughes during two morning events at the Richmondtown branch library. Poet, journalist, and actor David St. John Mills of Playwrights' Preview-Urban Stages starred in a one-man show featuring excerpts from the poetry of Hughes' many works, and followed with an opportunity for the students to ask questions about the life of Hughes. On another morning, the author/poet Tony Medina (*Love to Langston, Bum Rush the Page*, and *DeShawn Days*) and

Table 1. Young Adult Demographics

Ethnicity 2001–2002

School	% Caucasian	% African-American	% Hispanic	% Asian and other
IS 2	68.2	7.6	16.3	7.9
IS 49	20.2	43.1	30.4	6.4
IS 61	29.4	38.9	26.1	5.7

Free Lunch Eligibility 2002

School	%
IS 2	38.8
IS 49	74.4
IS 61	60.2

State and City Test Results in English Language Arts 2002

School	% meeting standards	% far below standards
IS 2	35.0	11.5
IS 49	19.6	24
IS 61	29.2	12.8

storyteller Joyce Parr, a member of Staten Island's literary karaoke group Staten Island Out LOUD, shared their enthusiasm for Langston Hughes' work. Both spoke at length about their reactions to Hughes work and how they are pursuing their own dreams.

Following the first visit to the library, students proceeded to the farm for planting cabbage, peas, and radishes. Following the second visit to the library, students harvested their crops and donated them to Staten Island's Project Hospitality Food Pantry. Students at one of the schools also held a food drive to provide further assistance.

Activities at school varied with the different classes. Some read Hughes's poems and short stories, others read and wrote about his life. All were given a packet full of materials developed by NYPL and the Staten Island Historical Society. These included a "Staten Island Then and Now" sheet, which asked students to compare the Staten Island of 1922 with today; for example, top songs, bestselling books, and racial diversity. There is also an exercise that took real help-wanted ads from some 1922 editions of the daily newspaper, *Staten Island Advance*, which listed racial preferences for different positions, and asked students about their reactions to the ads.

Staff and Volunteers

Staff	Hours:
One supervising librarian	105
One supervising librarian	8
Two administrative associates	8
One assistant coordinator of young adult services	4
Total	**125**

Budget

Central NYPL funds support special events for teens: Cost per staff hours:

Supervising librarian (CLASP)	$35.00
Supervising librarian (CLASP)	$30.53
Administrative associate (CLASP)	$19.56
Administrative associate (CLASP)	$19.19
Assistant coordinator of young adult services	$43.05
Honorarium for author (Tony Medina)	$300.00
Honorarium for Playwrights' Preview/ Urban Stages (David St. John Mills)	$200.00
Honorarium for storyteller (Joyce Parr)	$150.00
Total	**$797.33**

Evaluation

Participating teachers and librarians are currently completing their formal evaluations of this program. All teachers involved have requested to participate again, and the program will expand to include more classes.

Impact of the Program

Very little is known about Langston Hughes' sojourn on Staten Island from June to September 1922. Already a published poet at the age of twenty, Hughes abandoned his studies at Columbia University after only one year. When seeking employment in Manhattan, he encountered racial discrimination and was forced to look elsewhere in New York. Hughes moved to Staten Island in response to an advertisement for farm workers, as noted in his autobiography, *The Big Sea* (Hill & Wang, 1993).

Langston Hughes' poetry is very inspirational and accessible to young adults. In dealing with very real issues, such as poverty and racism, Hughes never loses his sense that things can be made better. There is no better example of success than his own life, rising from a poor farm worker to one of the great writers of the twentieth century. Very often students have a hard time seeing how the writings of people in other times and places have any connection to their own lives. By demonstrating that Langston Hughes lived and struggled not far from where the students now live, and by allowing the students to actually do the same work that Hughes did on Staten Island, it is hoped that the connections between Hughes' writing and the lives of the students will become clearer. We also hope that the success of this program will raise awareness among other schools and teachers to the fact that Langston Hughes has a local connection and that they will include this information in their classes.

A fringe benefit of this project was bringing two of Staten Island's major cultural institutions to work more closely on a project than they ever had before. The success of this collaboration is just the beginning. Much of the information obtained for this program has never been published before, and it is scheduled to appear in the next issue of the historical society's publication, *The Staten Island Historian*. NYPL is also working with Staten Island Community Television to produce a video for next year's program that will introduce the story of Hughes on Staten Island to a new group of students. There are also many other interesting figures from Staten Island's history—Paul Zindel and Henry David Thoreau, to name two—who could provide the basis for future collaborations.

For More Information

Andrew Wilson
Supervising Youth Services Librarian
NYPL Connecting Libraries and Schools Program
5 Central Ave.
Staten Island, NY 10310
(718) 720-9190
(718) 442-9744 (fax)
ahwilson@nypl.org

Poetry Alive!

Robert W. Cranston Library, Pleasant Valley High School, Chico, Calif.

Target Audience

High school students

Program Description

Poetry Alive is an exciting day filled with students reading their personal poetry or poetry from others,

musicians performing as the audience arrives and exits, and community members modeling poetry as a form of expression used by all ages. It is held every April during National Poetry Month in the Pleasant Valley High School (PVHS) library. The audience consists of students, faculty, and community members. Each class period approximately two hundred students arrive to either read or listen. By the end of the day, more than twelve hundred students have been part of the celebration of poetry and poets. This event has occurred for twelve consecutive years, evolving from being primarily community-driven to now being almost exclusively student-driven. Artwork celebrating literature is displayed in the library at the same time, and for the last three years this event has preceded the joint public/school library Teen Poetry Night held at a coffee shop.

Sponsoring Institution

Located in northern California, PVHS is a four-year, accredited high school. The student population has averaged around 2,150 over the last three years and comes from a variety of ethnic and cultural backgrounds. In addition, it is one of only a few schools in California with an International Baccalaureate program. The library media center is considered one of the top facilities in the north state, with more than one hundred student computer workstations and a collection of more than twenty thousand items from books, art prints, books on tape, CDs, videos, DVDs, and realia. One full-time library media teacher is employed, with one full-time clerical position shared by two individuals. The tenets of Information Power (www.ala.org/aaslTemplate.cfm?Section=informationpowerbook) are used as the basis for programming that occurs in the library with a heavy focus on classroom teacher/library media teacher collaboration. A variety of materials and individualized instruction for classes is our goal.

Young Adult Demographics

See table 2.

Program Participants

All PVHS students, grades nine through twelve, are designated for the audience. The focus group is often the English classes, specifically the creative writing classes; however, social studies, art, and special education classes also attend. After determining which classes have students interested in reading poetry, class sign ups are taken on a first-come, first-serve basis. Unfortunately, due to space limitations, many interested classes are unable to attend.

Each period, the library has at least 150 students attend from scheduled classes. In addition there are 30 passes given out to individual students who request them so they may attend as part of the audience or read.

Table 2.

Primary Language of Students

Language	Ninth grade	Tenth grade	Eleventh grade	Twelfth grade
English	469	475	482	449
Spanish	24	23	21	22
Hmong	21	16	19	14
Chinese	0	2	3	1
Vietnamese	0	1	1	1
Arabic	1	2	2	2
German	1	1	1	1
Other	3	7	2	5

Categorical and Specialized Program Enrollment

Program	Ninth grade M	Ninth grade F	Tenth grade M	Tenth grade F	Eleventh grade M	Eleventh grade F	Twelfth grade M	Twelfth grade F
Advancement via Individual Determination (AVID)	16	19	0	0	0	0	0	0
Honors English	42	56	46	76	0	0	0	0
Honors math	1	0	1	2	25	26	5	3
Honors science	1	0	37	45	0	0	0	0
Advanced placement	0	0	1	1	92	120	75	100
International Baccalaureate	0	0	1	1	92	120	75	100
Free/reduced lunch status	45	46	36	25	38	27	23	18
Aid to Families with Dependent Children (AFDC) Status	11	8	19	16	23	22	20	21

Language Proficiency Numbers

Classifications	Ninth grade	Tenth grade	Eleventh grade	Twelfth grade	Total
English language learners (ELL in ESL classes)	2	4	3	1	10
Limited English proficient (All ELL)	39	35	34	27	135
Fluent English proficient (FEP)	14	16	14	18	62
Reclassified FEP's (R-FEP)	0	0	0	0	0

Approximately thirty to forty students read during each period. Conservatively, 1,210 students participate during the day; however, a realistic estimate is closer to 1,350 students attending.

Youth Participation

Students on the planning committee are responsible for a variety of tasks, and these are typically geared to their interests or strengths. Options include publicity, master of ceremonies, recruiting other students to read, serving as back-up readers in case we have additional time, arranging the reservation for the facility and its subsequent setup, and organization of the overall program. Students also provide input on changes and modifications that should be made to the program. When planning the next year's day, students review the evaluations submitted to help determine what changes should be implemented. Student readers comprise all but thirty minutes of the day's events. The Poets in the Schools provide modeling and an example of poetry throughout one's life.

Staff and Volunteers

There is a committee of teachers and students who help plan and organize the day. Typically five teachers participate and students join the committee. Frequently, two students volunteer. Other volunteers include poets from the Poets in the Schools program, who volunteer their time to read during part of two periods.

Budget

Funding needs are very minimal. The only expenses incurred are the newsletters sent with the attached sign up form, gifts for the Poets in the Schools, and miniature candy bars for students who read their poetry.

Item	Cost	Total
Notecards for Poets in the Schools	$5.00 each	$10.00
Candy for student poets	two bags at Costco	$18.00
Newsletter copies	120 copies @ $.03	$3.60
Total Cost:		**$31.60**

Typically the funding for candy and gifts comes from the personal budget of the library media teacher; however, for the past two years the library and the California Scholarship Federation have collaborated on fundraising to purchase the gifts for the Poets in the Schools and for the candy. The photocopy cost comes from the site library budget.

Evaluation

Evaluation of the program is vital. Evaluation forms are randomly sent to two of the classes that are part of the audience for each period the program was held. The evaluations are overwhelmingly positive year after year, yet thoughtful comments sometimes suggest modifications we can make. Many students would like an additional day of Poetry Alive. These evaluations are examined during the current year and again at planning meetings the following year. Several modifications have been made to the program based on these evaluations. Since space considerations limit the number of participants, this data does not change from year to year in any appreciable way.

Impact of the Program

Poetry Alive honors students whose talents are not traditionally recognized by the community. Frequently, students must be athletes to be featured in the school publications. Poetry Alive showcases students and allows them to be acknowledged by their peers and teachers for academic achievement and for their creativity. Students are applauded by their peers and noted in the school newspaper, the library Web site, and on the school annual video. In addition, students are recognized while on campus by teachers and students for their contribution. The greatest impact on students is the fact that the stereotype of poetry not being a cool thing is completely shattered. Throughout the twelve years of this program, it has grown to be one of the major events at this school that students eagerly anticipate.

For More Information

Linda E. Elliott
Library Media Teacher
Pleasant Valley High School
1475 East Ave.
Chico, CA 95926
(530) 879-5197
(530) 879-5263 (fax)
lelliott@pvchico.org

6. Miscellany

The programs in this chapter all target a specific subset of the young adult population with the exception of the Young Adult Services Institute, which targeted library staff members. Earphone English aims to improve the communication skills of English language learners by providing them with slower-paced audiobooks and a forum in which to discuss the stories they've listened to. The Home Pages home school book club brings home-schooled students into the library to discuss books that they might not otherwise have read as a part of their regular curriculum. The Teen Parent Program teaches pregnant and parenting teen mothers the importance of reading to their children. Finally, the Young Adult Services Institute provided a series of staff development workshops on various aspects of young adult services that inspired the creation of young adult spaces and the improvement of young adult programming and collection development in its library system.

Earphone English

Berkeley (Calif.) Public Library

Target Audience

Middle school and high school English language learners

Program Description

Earphone English provides English language learning (ELL) teens in Berkeley secondary schools with facilitated discussions of audio books available for them to borrow on a free-choice basis. Exposure to high-interest books in an accessible format, the modeling of English pronunciation and inflections, the opportunity to participate in developmentally appropriate critical discussions, and the presence of librarians with whom to discuss informational concerns beyond literature are the hallmarks of this three-year-old program. Weekly school-based meetings give participants the opportunity to talk about books to which they have listened and collect new listening and reading suggestions to suit their emerging interests. Participants' communication skills improve quickly, as does their appreciation of their own abilities to be successful with English. Interest in exploring the library on their own is whetted by the experience the teens have with the visiting librarians, who provide guidance toward the use of both school and public libraries.

Sponsoring Institution

Berkeley Public Library (BPL), through a staff that includes 4.5 FTE teen librarians, provides collections and services to the city's five thousand teens through a variety of media and programs at five locations and through various outreach projects. Materials and programming at BPL include offerings in a spectrum of non-English languages. The central library is a block from the city's only public high school. BPL staff members work directly and collaboratively with school librarians at the high school and middle schools. The partnership between BPL's teen services and the secondary schools' ELL departments has been developed through a decade of class visits, special programs at BPL, and BPL outreach to ELL students to solicit their participation in more broadly targeted programming, such as summer reading programs. Teens, including those enrolled in ELL classes, work at BPL both in paid and volunteer capacities.

Young Adult Demographics

While the Berkeley Unified School District's three hundred sixth- through twelfth-grade students identified as needing ELL support represent more than thirty home languages, Earphone English participants in the middle school grades are predominantly Spanish-speaking, and those in the high school grades speak a broad mix of Asian, African, and European languages. Those participating at the middle school have intermediate English

language speaking skills and varying degrees of English literacy skills. At the high school level, participants include ELL students with minimal to superior speaking and reading skills.

We have determined, through interviews and observation, that most ELL students have little previous experience with public libraries and come from families uncertain of how to access library services. Fewer than 10 percent of Earphone English participants have had any previous experience of someone reading aloud to them anything more than a passage or a poem. Like the larger population of Berkeley adolescents, there is great range in the ELL population in regard to socioeconomic circumstances, family construct, and length of stay in the community. Some participants are attending school for the first time in some years after living in refugee camps, while others are here only for a year while a parent does research at the University of California.

Program Participants

Earphone English targets ELL teens, a group comprising 8 percent of the city's school enrollment. At the high school level (grades nine through twelve), Earphone English is offered as a voluntary activity, while at the middle school level (grades six through eight), ELL students in specific classrooms participate in Earphone English as part of their curriculum. In both cases, a small number of non-ELL students participate in the program because of friendships with ELL students (at the high school) or intersecting classroom assignments (in the case of the middle school). Non-ELL teens account for fewer than 6 percent of the participants, who currently number 125.

Youth Participation

Earphone English began as a pilot project among a Berkeley High School ELL teacher, four of her students, and a BPL teen services librarian early in 2001. From the outset, high school participants have contributed ideas about program format; devised and produced publicity targeting their peers; initiated special group activities, including potlucks, movie outings, picnics, and mehndi parties; and helped develop the means to circulate the program's materials. They have written about their experiences with the program at the end of each school year, and they have allowed themselves to be interviewed by observers from the state English Language Literacy Intensive (ELLI) oversight office. During the first two years of the program, few boys availed themselves of participation; this third year, many boys are participating at both the middle and high schools, apparently due to the perception that this is a cool activity, a blessing only the teens themselves could foment among their peers.

Staff and Volunteers

One public librarian works with the high school program, in which eighty teens—50 percent of the school's ELL student body—are active, meeting with the librarian two to four times a month. An ELL teacher hosts the high school program in her classroom weekly at a lunch period, and usually attends group discussions. Two or three other ELL teachers attend the discussions sporadically. A former ELL student and Earphone English founding member (now a community college student) provides clerical assistance to the high school program. High school participants listen to the audiobooks, with or without accompanying print texts as each chooses, on their personal time. A second public librarian works with three middle school ELL classes, a total of forty-five students, on a weekly basis. There, Earphone English is a component of the classroom curriculum. Middle school teachers support the program by allowing participants to listen to their audiobooks on personal cassette players during sustained silent reading periods.

With input from ELL teachers and the school sites' librarians, the two BPL librarians providing this program in the schools select audiobooks for the Earphone English collection (now totaling about 450 volumes) and develop brief booktalks with which to introduce teens to new titles. Once circulated, titles are promoted to Earphone English participants by other participants as part of the weekly discussion.

Budget

This year, Earphone English is partially underwritten by an ELLI grant from the California State Library. The grant funds pay for audiobooks, ancillary programming at the public library, and the additional ten hours per week both of the public librarians together need to accomplish Earphone English duties. The ancillary programs target Earphone English participants and encourage them to bring friends and family to the public library to explore crafts and theater and obtain library cards so as to use library computers and check out materials for home use. While the ELLI money has helped in particular to build a large collection of audiobooks and to be able to supply any participant in need with a personal cassette player and batteries (instructional materials that we budget at $20,000 for this year), the program was begun with no special budget and will continue to be offered at the end of this grant period. The library now has a wide and deep audio book collection that can be augmented more gradually with the teen services materials budget and Friends of the Library grants in future years. Staff support at the library also allows for the exchange of public service desk hours for a portion of the time needed for school site visits.

Evaluation

In the first year Earphone English was offered, participants—including teens, the ELL teacher, and the public librarian—offered each other direct feedback in order to shape the program. After only six weeks, the teens were observed by a kindergarten teacher to have become more effective oral readers in the kindergarten work-study positions they each held. We also heard from the high school librarian that there was heightened interest among ELL students in asking for assistance and borrowing materials from the school library. In the subsequent two years, evaluation has included these types of observations as well as the granting agency's requirement of reporting standardized test scores. Because public library staff lack the expertise to interpret standardized test scores meaningfully, and ELL students participate only irregularly in standardized testing sessions in the district, this has not seemed to be a meaningful evaluation method for determining the library's or the teen participants' desired outcomes.

Measurements that do seem useful to us, however, include the sharp increase in library use and communication skills exhibited by Earphone English participants. In the past year, 20 percent of Berkeleyans over the age of thirteen seeking first-time library cards have identified themselves as ELL students. Earphone English participants have begun to participate in other school activities, both in the realms of political activism and social clubs; more than 50 percent of the high school Earphone English group belong to at least one school-level organization that is not ELL-targeted, up from fewer than 10 percent who did three years ago.

ELL students participating in Earphone English have brought family members and friends to the public library to participate in age-appropriate programming, obtain library cards, and translate when these friends and family members have concerns about library fees and other sensitive issues. Both the school libraries and the public library locations have witnessed increased interest on the parts of Earphone English participants in working in the library; ELL students are currently employed at two BPL branches and work as proctors in the high school library.

Circulation of teen audio book materials at the public library has risen dramatically since the inception of this program (about a 40 percent rise in the past twelve months). ELL teens are considerably more vocal, too, in requesting print materials in a variety of home languages, indicating to us that they have developed a new understanding of the public library as rightfully *theirs*.

Middle school teachers report that nearly every Earphone English participant in their charge successfully completes a book within the first month of participation, an often first-time experience that leads to the desire to find another good book and to improved attitudes about books and reading as well as about class participation. Both middle and high school students meet new as well as familiar scenarios and values in the audiobooks' stories, material that incites discussion about such cultural realities as civil rights, crises of sexual identity, and other matters that are as new to some participants as is the experience of speaking, reading, and hearing English. Earphone English discussions tend to include questions about American culture, analyses of audiobook narrators' voice qualities, and, of course, opinions about the book as a piece of literature.

Program recidivism seems to indicate that participants can grow and enjoy growing within the program. Earphone English participants have requested and received summer meetings each year, convened at a public library branch, and several ELL students who have tested out of ELL-supported classes continue to attend Earphone English regularly. The attendance of participants, their families, and their friends at ancillary library programs demonstrates the connection participants have drawn between the school-based program and more general reliance on the library as a valuable resource.

Impact of the Program

Earphone English provides ELL teens with the opportunity to discover the joy of books by providing them with audio format titles specifically written for teens or with which teens traditionally find connection and allowing them to hear English spoken well; to share their opinions, in English, about the materials to which they listen as individuals; and to explore the library as a new way of having access to both desirable information and the free use of materials and technology. Earphone English participants enjoy the attention they receive from library staff as well as the new relationship they are able to build with English language books and literature. They begin to speak more effectively in English, seek books that interest them both for listening and for print reading, obtain library cards, and encourage other family members—both younger and older—to enter and use the public library, now that it has been demystified by their involvement in its services and wares. Teachers report improved dispositions in class and more effective engagement in both the peer group and broader community on the parts of participants. The program seems to work as an entrée into American civic life as well as providing the personal fulfillment of meeting new challenges in a new culture.

For More Information

Francisca Goldsmith
Berkeley Public Library
2090 Kittredge St.
Berkeley, CA 94704
(510) 981-6139
(510) 981-6246 (fax)
frg1@berkeley.ca.us

Home Pages Home School Book Club

Laramie County Library System, Cheyenne, Wyo.

Target Audience

Middle, junior high, and senior high home school students

Program Description

Home Pages, a young adult home school book club began at the Laramie County Library System (LCLS) in January 2002, provides opportunities for home school students and their families to participate in activities that support home school curricula, including book discussion groups, author visits, and special programs. Home Pages was created through an identified need to offer programming for home-schooled teens in grades seven through twelve that supplemented their home curricula, familiarized them with literature outside of their normal studies, and introduced them to library services and materials. Home Pages meets for an hour each month starting in September and ending in May. During the meeting, the participants discuss the selected title and compare it to other selections they have read. When an author or guest speaker visits, the young adults explore the process of writing at a professional level or create artwork related to a specific title.

Sponsoring Institution

LCLS serves the 81,607 citizens of Laramie County through a central library in Cheyenne, two rural branches, homebound services, and a bookmobile. The library system employs thirty-one FTEs. The greater Cheyenne area has a population of approximately 68,000 people. LCLS enjoys stable funding due to support from the people of Laramie County and the Laramie County Commissioners. The library system houses a collection of approximately 260,000 books. LCLS has an extremely active youth advisory board with eighteen members and a small to moderately sized young adult area with a growing collection of teen materials, including nonfiction, graphic novels, magazines, and fiction collections. LCLS began programming specifically targeted at home school families in 2001, offering library skills classes and annual home school forums.

Young Adult Demographics

According to the 2000 U.S. Census, Cheyenne has a total of 7,438 children between ten and nineteen years of age, the primary age range for young adult services. The ethnic makeup of this group was 84 percent Caucasian, 10 percent Hispanic, 3 percent African-American, and 3 percent other, including Asian and Native American.

Wyoming requires home school families to report their activities to the state, but many families who choose to educate their children outside the system are also leery of government intervention and may not be in compliance with these regulations. Laramie County School District 1 reports a total of 312 students currently being home-schooled in the district, but this number is not reliable. Further complicating the matter, home school students over the age of sixteen are not required to be registered with the local district at all. LCLS currently has about 150 home school families on a mailing list, representing only a portion of the total potential home school families in the county.

Program Participants

Cheyenne has a large number of home school families representing a broad range of social, religious, and political choices for educating children outside of public schools. However, the overwhelming majority of those seen at the library are choosing to home school specifically for religious reasons, primarily Christian. Home-schooled teens offer a particular challenge to the library in that their reading levels can vary widely, their curricula often dictate specific older titles for reading instruc-

tion, and they are frequently reluctant to read outside of genres considered safe for Christian teens.

In creating Home Pages, the challenge has been to not only choose materials that would be appropriate for curricular support and accepted by teens and their parents, but also to find ways to make the program interesting and engaging for this particular group. Home Pages is limited to material available in paperback, and we must screen all choices for profanity, sexual content, witchcraft, and other potentially objectionable topics. While trying to occasionally push the envelope with some titles, LCLS also tries to justify selections based on literary merit and application to relevant curricular topics, such as racism, war, or exploration. Home Pages is promoted to teens through a local home school newsletter as well as through the library's existing home school mailing list, internal flyers, and local media.

Average attendance at Home Pages is between ten and fifteen young adults in grades seven through twelve. The group meets once a month, and the number of participants has been consistent at ten to twelve. Total attendance since the program started in January 2002 is 177 teens.

Youth Participation

The Home Pages participants have input on the titles chosen for each session. They also read and discuss each of the selections. During the author and guest visits, the young adults actively participate in the discussion or activity. Routinely, two titles were offered, and most participants chose to read both selections.

Regular input from Home Pages participants and their parents continues to make the program better. For example, when Home Pages first met, students in third through twelfth grade met as one group. After a couple of meetings, the group decided it would function better if the groups were split into grades three through six and grades seven through twelve. At the last meeting of the year, Home Pages participants, their parents, and LCLS staff evaluate the success and failures of the previous year. The evaluation includes questions about the programs and books that were presented at each of the meetings. This also provides an opportunity for all to describe what they would like to read during the next year.

Staff and Volunteers

The Home Pages staff consists primarily of the young adult specialist, who is responsible for planning, implementing, and managing the program. Additional assistance comes from the youth and outreach services manager and the library's public relations specialist. Three additional youth and outreach services library staff members play an integral role in overall home school programming at LCLS through program development and staffing for events. Volunteer support comes from both teens and adults, depending on the program and its timing. Many home school students are volunteers at the library and just naturally help out at programs they are attending, making the need for additional volunteers unnecessary.

Budget

Support for Home Pages is provided through the LCLS's young adult programming funds, staff salaries, in-kind donations, printing budget, and the Laramie County Library Foundation (LCLF), which solicits private donations. The following figures are estimated costs for a single year of the program, with staff costs being based on an hourly rate derived from annual salaries plus 30 percent for benefits where applicable. The facility costs are based on a flat rate the library charges for meeting room use to cover utilities and maintenance. Food, books, postage, and printing are estimates based on an annual basis of nine programs a year (one a month on average, summers off). Performer fees are based on the percentage of the program provide presented to the group.

Personnel

Public relations specialist	25 hours x $15	$375
Youth and outreach services manager	20 hours x $20	$400
YA specialist (1x)	45 hours x $15	$675
Youth and outreach services staff	15 hours x $15	$225
Performer fees	three per year (fees vary)	$750

Supplies and Materials

Books	author visits, giveaways	$250
Printing	fliers, postcards, calendars	$1,000
Postage	postcards (bulk mailing)	$100
Refreshments	lunches, snacks, dessert	$400
Facilities	$25 per room use x 12	$300
Total		**$4475**

Evaluation

Evaluation of Home Pages occurs throughout the year, and a formal evaluation is completed at the last meeting. The evaluation is an opportunity for participants, their parents, and the staff to reflect on the number and kind of books read, the hour and number of times they met, and the kinds of programs presented.

Prior to January 2002, the programs LCLS provided to home school families were limited to a fall meeting, where parents were introduced to the services provided by the library, and a library skills class for home-schooled students in second through twelfth grades. Younger students primarily utilized the class.

Impact of the Program

Home Pages provides educational support to home school parents and students while encouraging them to expand their reading horizons beyond their set curricula. The program is intended as a supplement and as an enhancement, as well as an opportunity for these young adults to socialize with peers and explore ideas beyond their own home environment. Home-schooled teens in particular need to build relationships with adults outside of their homes and to connect with other teens in the community. Home Pages gives these teens a forum of their own, as they are often the quieter participants in larger young adult events open to the entire community. The program also provides a welcome respite for home school parents, who are often teaching several grades simultaneously and greatly appreciate the public library contributing to their child's education.

Home Pages supports home school curricula primarily through historical fiction titles, and it occasionally provides opportunities for students to explore some aspect of the story through a hands-on activity. The most recent selection was *A Single Shard* (Yearling, 2003) by Linda Sue Park. A guest artist was invited to the library to demonstrate pottery making and give students an opportunity to try it out. Other books read over the past year and a half include *Across Five Aprils* (Berkley, 1987) by Irene Hunt, *Moccasin Trail* (Puffin, 1986) by Eloise Jarvis McGraw, and *The True Confessions of Charlotte Doyle* (HarperTrophy, 1992) by Avi.

Additionally, participants have been able to attend a number of special home school-only events offered during the school day that included an author luncheon and private book signing with Elizabeth Levy, a song writing workshop with Gary Dulabaum, author talks

with Debbie Dadey and Ron Woods, and an aboriginal science program with Paul Taylor. Frequently these special programs are done in conjunction with the two younger home school book clubs LCLS sponsors, as home school teens rarely have the same aversion to mixing with younger children that most young adults experience due to their naturally multi-aged learning environments.

For More Information

Amelia Shelley
Laramie County Library System
2800 Central Ave.
Cheyenne, WY 82001
(307) 634-3561, ext. 151
(307) 634-2082 (fax)
ashelley@larm.lib.wy.us

Teen Parent Project

Fresno County (Calif.) Public Library

Target Audience

Pregnant teens and teen parents

Program Description

The Teen Parent Project was developed through a coalition of three librarians, the University Medical Center teen parent educator, and two Fresno Unified School District Parent and Child Education Program (PACE) coordinators, and is coordinated by the Fresno County Public Library (FCPL). The coalition created a survey that was administered to PACE program participants to determine what programs and services the library could provide that teen parents would find most useful. In response, workshops were designed to share the importance of reading to young children and the library's reading and programming resources relevant to parenting, teen interests, and life skills. Infant and toddler programs that parents could duplicate at home were modeled at the PACE childcare centers. Workshops and infant and toddler programs have also been offered at local hospitals; the Sanctuary, a shelter for runaway/throwaway teens; and at the Valley Teen Parent Conference. In addition, teen parent collections have been created at five libraries.

Sponsoring Institution

FCPL serves a diverse population, both urban and rural, through a central library, thirty branches, and two bookmobiles. Its population exceeds 764,800 and is increasing rapidly; 11 percent of this figure is made up of young adults age twelve to eighteen. Despite this large population group, prior to 2001 services to teens were virtually nonexistent. In April 2001, a young adult department, consisting of a YA services coordinator and a YA specialist, was created to develop and oversee all county services to teens age fourteen to eighteen. Three YA specialists were hired to work in the large regional libraries. All branches are required to provide a level of service to young adults, and ten branches have generalists that regularly provide programming for this age group as well. Input for service and programs is provided by teens through five teen councils, and through our library teen Web site, www.fresnolibrary. org/teen.

Young Adult Demographics

The young adults in Fresno County, ages twelve to eighteen, number 84,128, which is approximately 11 percent of the overall population. The group is 44 percent Latino, 40 percent Caucasian, 15 percent Asian, 5 percent African-American, and 1 percent Native American. According to *County Health Status Profiles 2000* (California Department of Health Services, 2000), 30 percent of teens in the area do not graduate from high school, and poverty rates for young people average 30 percent. In 1998, California's teen pregnancy rate dropped to an average of 53 births per 1,000 teens, ages fifteen to nineteen (California Report Card, 2000). Fresno County teen birth rates ranks well above the state average, with 83.9 per 1,000 teens (age fifteen to nineteen) in 1997 according to the *California County Data Book, 1999* (Children Now, 1999). Most fathers of children born to teen mothers are not teens themselves; 63 percent are 20 years and older. Eighty-four percent of teen fathers live apart from their children.

Program Participants

The Teen Parent Project was designed for pregnant or parenting teens and those who care for them. Since the beginning of the project we have conducted workshops for approximately four hundred teens. Through our workshop and booth at the Valley Teen Parent Conference we were able to put materials into the hands of more than 1,100 teen parents throughout the San Joaquin Valley. The Teen Parent Collection is available beyond FCPL jurisdiction through a cooperative collection sharing agreement among San Joaquin Valley Library System member libraries and through interlibrary loan.

Youth Participation

Members of the Cedar-Clinton Branch Library Teen Council 2000–2001 were invited to participate on the coalition. Teen councils also assisted by stuffing library bags with booklists, pencils, library card applications, and other pertinent items. Input on the development of

relevant programming and services was received from more than one hundred students involved in the PACE program through the survey developed by the coalition.

Staff and Volunteers

Two young adult librarians are involved in this project; they conduct the workshops and promote the service in the community. Two more librarians assist at the annual Valley Teen Parent Conference by staffing a library booth.

Budget

The original funding for this program was provided through a Partnerships for Change Implementation Grant through the California State Library, allowing an operating budget of $10,000. These expenses included the purchase of materials for the Teen Parent Collection for the program's pilot site, the survey costs, workshop materials, and door prizes. Regular staff hours were used by FCPL. After the pilot project, $6,000 was allocated from the library's regular young adult materials budget to expand the teen parent collection to four more sites.

Evaluation

At every workshop the library staff conducts, an evaluation sheet is provided for attendees. These are read by the young adult department staff, and any suggestions offered are seriously considered. Overall, these evaluations have been positive, with many attendees stating that they "never knew how much the library had" for them, and "I will start reading to my child[ren] now!" Circulation of the teen parent collection is monitored on a regular basis, and figures indicate a steady increase since its introduction in the library. Both teens and other community agencies that serve the target group use the collection. The steady request for workshops also indicates a community desire and need to continue the project. In the first year, the young adult services staff conducted three workshops at the high school sites, four at University Medical Center, and one at the Valley Teen Parent Conference. In the 2002–2003 school year, approximately the same number of programs were conducted, and an additional workshop site was added.

Impact of the Program

Teen mothers are less likely to finish high school and more likely to live in poverty than other teens. Babies born to teen mothers are more likely to spend a portion of their lives on welfare. In light of these facts, this population needs the support of public services and resources. The library and its staff are best qualified to provide and model read-aloud activities. Library resources can help to diminish the future social and educational risks among teens and their children. Programs such as the Teen Parent Project contribute to the future learning success of these parents' unborn and young children. The ability to read is the single most important educational activity toward academic success, and reading aloud to children is the most important activity for building the knowledge required for eventual reading success. The Teen Parent Project introduces teen parents to the tools necessary to foster reading skills and enjoyment in their children. The hoped for end result is better-equipped children who achieve greater success in school and break the cycle of pregnancy, dropping out of school, and poverty for these families.

For More Information

Kelley Worman
Fresno County Public Library
2420 Mariposa St.
Fresno, CA 93721
(559) 488-3205
(559) 488-1971 (fax)
kelley.worman@fresnolibrary.org

Young Adult Services Institute: Serving San Joaquin Valley Teens in the Twenty-First Century

San Joaquin Valley Library System, Fresno, Calif.

Target Audience

Library staff

Program Description

The Young Adult Services Institute was a two-year project of the San Joaquin Valley Library System (SJVLS) that consisted of training staff and creating model teen spaces and interagency programming. The project began with a needs assessment. Teen library users and nonusers and teen councils were surveyed and, based on the resulting data, mission statements, long-range goals, and action plans for teen library service were developed. Six consultants, known for expertise in their fields, were hired to present twelve workshops for library staff. The quarterly workshops addressed specific topics related to young adult service, such as library materials, the psychology of young adults, customer service, marketing and public relations, teen library spaces, and collabora-

tive programming with agencies outside of the library. Model building spaces were created in two libraries, and each SJVLS jurisdiction implemented interagency programs with two new partners.

Sponsoring Institution

SJVLS is a cooperative network consisting of nine public library jurisdictions: Fresno County Public Library; Kern County Library; Coalinga-Huron District Library; Kings County Library; Madera County Library; Mariposa County Library; Porterville Public Library; Tulare County Library; and Tulare Public Library. Collectively, these systems represent one hundred branch libraries. Only one of the participating jurisdictions boasts young adult specialists, including a young adult services coordinator. Most branches are required to provide some level of service to young adults, so the majority of this work is being done either by children's services librarians or generalists. Input for service and programs is provided by teens through teen councils and two library systems' teen Web sites (www.fresnolibrary.org/teen and www.kerncountylibrary.org/teensite.html).

Young Adult Demographics

SJVLS serves a diverse and rapidly increasing population, both urban and rural, of approximately 2,189,878 people; 11 percent of this figure is made up of young adults age twelve to eighteen (approximately 240,887 youth) according to the U.S. Census county estimates for 2001. The demographics of this group are 44 percent Latino, 40 percent Caucasian, 15 percent Asian, 5 percent African-American, and 1 percent Native American. According to *County Health Status Profiles 2000* (California Department of Health Services, 2000), 30 percent of teens in the area do not graduate from high school, and poverty rates for young people average 30 percent.

Program Participants

The institute was open to all interested library staff. Participation was mandatory for all young adult specialists, and optional to all others. Approximately two hundred staff members from the jurisdictions participated in the various workshops and grant objectives.

Staff and Volunteers

The young adult services coordinator of the Fresno County Public Library served as the project manager. One SJVLS staff person assisted with various tasks on a part-time basis.

Budget

The Young Adult Services Institute was funded through a Library Services and Technology Act grant by the

California State Library, providing $188,720. In-kind monies were provided by SJVLS for salaries and materials. In-kind salaries were based on twenty hours per month of each jurisdiction's representative's time, at an average cost of $16 per hour, and cost to send staff members to eight (two per topic) training sessions at eight hours per session. In-kind salaries also included the cost of the project manager spending approximately ten hours per week on the project at an approximate cost of $16 per hour. In-kind library materials cost was based on each jurisdiction adding approximately thirty-five to forty items to the YA collection at approximately $15 per item. Equipment costs for two model space plans were approximately $15,000, which allowed for two simple, aesthetic makeovers that other branches could emulate.

Evaluation

Circulation statistics of young adult materials, increase or decrease in teen library use, and participation in library programming were monitored by participating jurisdictions and their branches. All jurisdictions reported on a quarterly basis that circulation figures of YA materials continued to rise throughout the entire grant project by a range of 10–19 percent. Collections were improved through an increase of new and pertinent titles and through better weeding of older and irrelevant materials. More teens were getting library cards and attending programs. Several branches indicated an increase in services and programs offered at their site. For example, Fresno County Public Library branches offered fifty-five programs for teens in 2000, but offered approximately three hundred programs throughout the 2002–2003 fiscal year. Six jurisdictions reported the creation or growth of teen councils and advisory groups, which led to more relevant service and an increase in platforms for teen feedback. Four jurisdictions reported expanded or first-time summer teen reading programs.

Each training session was evaluated by the participants. The first workshop, conducted by Patrick Jones on customized plans, was instrumental in igniting enthusiasm for serving young adults. This enthusiasm continued throughout the project, with no visible decrease in attendance at the workshops. Some of the workshops were better received than others, but the overall response was extremely positive. Many staff members expressed regret that they had missed earlier workshops once they began attending the institute.

Finally, a manual that covers all aspects of the institute was produced and distributed to all participating library systems to assist in the continued efforts of staff and for training new staff. The manual is available for purchase to all other interested libraries through the Fresno County Public Library.

Since the conclusion of the project, informal evaluation of the institute's success has continued through the quarterly meetings of the SJVLS Youth Services Committee. Jurisdictions have demonstrated an ongoing commitment to the mission and goals established during the first portion of the institute. Branches continue to develop new services and outreach to the target population, and they are still reporting continued success of their programming.

Impact of the Program

SJVLS libraries have long had a mission to provide quality service to all user groups. While SJVLS had historically provided quality service to children and adults, because of stretched financial and staff resources service to young adults (ages twelve to eighteen) had been largely ignored by the system libraries. Few libraries had professional young adult specialists, and only two branches had YA-specific rooms or spaces. Only a few libraries had conducted programming for teens, and all reported low attendance. Library jurisdictions had always purchased library materials for young adults, but collections remained small and inadequate. Through informal and formal data collection methods, it became evident that we needed to make our libraries teen friendly by creating teen-designated areas, purchasing collections that would entice and inspire teens to read and use the collection, and creating programming with other community agencies. Clearly, there was also a need to educate staff regarding the developmental needs and assets of young adults and to explore new ways of providing service in order to create opportunities for successful transition into adulthood. The Young Adult Services Institute attempted to do all of these things by training and educating staff in six key areas of exemplary library service. The results have been a positive dramatic shift in staff attitudes and an increase in programming and services throughout the San Joaquin Valley. Library staff has developed better understanding of teen interests and needs, resulting in greater rapport with their patrons. In turn, the improved relationships have increased teen use of the library and their understanding of what the library can mean in their lives. Young adult collections have improved, both in quality and quantity, through monies provided by the project, and now young adult spaces and shelving in branches are the norm rather than the exception.

For More Information

Kelley Worman
Fresno County Public Library
2420 Mariposa St.
Fresno, CA 93721
(559) 488-3205
(559) 488-1971 (fax)
kelley.worman@fresnolibrary.org

7. Summer Reading

This chapter showcases the wide variety of summer reading and related activities that can be offered by public libraries. Reading Rocks! relied on young adult input to improve its program marketing and selection of reading incentives. In addition to reading books, hundreds of teens volunteered to help keep the library's summer reading programs for all ages running smoothly. The RELAX.READ Book Blitz brought public school classes into the public library to entice them to participate in the summer reading program through presentations, book talks, displays, a rap performance, and photo and video booths that allowed teens to share the importance of reading in their lives. *Teen2Teen* took advantage of book reviews created by young adults during the summer reading program to create a booklet for other teens to use to select their reading. Teen Productions provided an alternative to a traditional summer reading program by offering a series of three-day intensive workshops on a variety of topics. Participants then went on to share the skills they had learned through other library programs and events throughout the summer.

Reading Rocks!

Naperville (Ill.) Public Library

Target Audience

Middle, junior high, and senior high school students

Program Description

In 2000, only 391 Naperville young adults participated in the summer reading program out of an estimated 20,438 in the ten- to nineteen-year-old age group (2000 U.S. Census). Using surveys for ages eleven to eighteen, it was determined that the library was not providing a program that appealed to local teens. The staff decided a complete overhaul of service to young adults was necessary.

The resulting 2001 and 2002 summer programs introduced the concept of rewards for reading 200, 400, 600, and so on, pages. Prize coupons for goods and services were solicited from businesses teens indicated they preferred. Snappy graphics were used on handouts, the registration tables were placed in prominent locations, and local celebrities were honorees at the ending raffle. Before the program began, library staff visited middle and high schools to give an infomercial to draw teen registrants to the young adult summer reading program, and hundreds of teen volunteers were recruited. The result was a 460 percent increase in participation in two years.

Sponsoring Institution

Located thirty miles west of Chicago in Illinois' designated high-tech research corridor, the Naperville Public Library serves a population of more than 133,000 in the fourth-largest city in Illinois. At the time of this summer reading program, the library was composed of the downtown Nichols Library and the southeast Naper Boulevard Library. A third library, serving the southwest quadrant of the city, opened in September 2003.

The residents of Naperville are well-educated and active library users. More than 60 percent of the residents age twenty-five and older have bachelor's degrees or higher. In fiscal year 2002–2003, the library was visited 1,261,430 times; 2,968,217 items were circulated; and 39,360 people attended 1,073 programs. For five years in a row, the library has been ranked number one in the country in its population class by Hennen's American Library Rating Service.

Young Adult Demographics

According to the 2000 Census, the median family income in Naperville is $88,771, compared to the United States average of $42,000. The average owner-occupied housing value is $245,200, compared to the United States. average of $119,000. Clearly, Naperville is a somewhat affluent community. Parents are well-educated, and their children are involved in many

The STARS (Summer Time Assistants Really Shine) manned the summer reading program desks in the children's and young adult areas of the two libraries. They answered questions, collected reading logs, and passed out prizes. They encouraged younger children and peers to read and to share their joy in reading. In 2002, STARS manned desks that would have required 4,009 staff hours and would have cost the library more than $58,000 in salaries ($14.48 x 4,009).

Reading Buddies combined junior high and high school readers one-on-one with younger elementary school readers. The pairs met once a week. Sometimes the older buddy read, sometime the younger buddy, and together they developed a time of sharing the joy of reading. The increase in participation from 2000 to 2002 was 130 percent for volunteers and 215 percent in hours. In 2002, 705 hours were volunteered to the Reading Buddies program. If staff had acted as Reading Buddies, it would have cost $10,215 in salaries ($14.48 x 705).

In 2002, the 121 teens who served as Buddies and the 283 STARS were rewarded with a dozen donuts compliments of Krispy Kreme and a pass to the Sci-Tech Museum. The successful program had a trickle-down effect—the adult summer reading program participation also increased 254 percent.

Staff and Volunteers

The Young Adult summer reading program committee included representatives from administration, children's, facilities, graphics, and information technology as well as adult and teen services departments. This nontraditional mix of opinions and points of view greatly enriched the resulting summer reading plan.

Budget

Teens wanted specific prizes awarded at each plateau reached. In addition to prizes from local establishments that teens enjoy, the survey indicated that teens wanted quality books as prizes. In previous years, boxed sets of YA books were ordered that were not always the most desired titles. In 2002, the librarians used the recommended reading lists from YALSA as a selection guide. This change resulted in increased participation at the various levels. Purchase of these books was possible from money generated from an ask letter sent to local businesses requesting funding for the summer reading program. In its inaugural year, the letter generated more than $4,000 in cash for the reading program, and more than $172,000 in coupons and prizes.

In 2002, the Chicago Fire professional soccer team began a two-year stint of playing their games at the North Central College campus in Naperville while their home venue, Soldier Field, underwent renovation. To further enhance the summer reading program, the library partnered with the Fire team to provide tickets to the games,

activities. With all that the teens are into, it is hard for the library to get their attention. The Reading Rocks! summer program did the trick.

According to the Illinois School Report Card, the high school drop-out rate for the Naperville schools was 0.55 percent, compared to 5.1 percent for the state of Illinois. The largest minority population is Asian/Pacific Islander, with 11.4 percent

Program Participants

The YA summer reading program is targeted toward teens aged eleven to eighteen. The changes implemented in the program resulted in an increase of participation from 391 in 2000 to 2,064 in 2001 (456 percent) and a 40 percent increase in YA fiction circulation.

Youth Participation

One of the most exciting aspects of the 2001 and 2002 YA summer reading programs was the quantity and quality of the teens recruited as volunteers. In 2001, 260 volunteered, and in 2002 83 of the 380 volunteers were returnees from the year before. All volunteers were required to attend a mandatory, hour-long orientation program in which logistics, proper dress, and customer service skills were emphasized. The volunteers were divided into two categories—STARS and Reading Buddies.

memorabilia, player appearances, and so on. Demarcus Beasley, international soccer star, did the drawing for the final summer reading program teen raffle.

In 2002 the library also partnered with the *Daily Herald* newspaper for a pilot Big Ticket reading program. The *Herald* secured free tickets to some of Chicago's biggest attractions, including Field Museum, Shedd Aquarium, Art Institute. When children, teens, and adults attained certain reading plateaus, they had their choice of these premium tickets. The teens and their parents loved the variety and the value of this program. However, it was a very labor-intensive project since each participant had a choice of numerous tickets, and decisions were not always made swiftly. The STARS volunteers were invaluable. If the library had to man the registration tables for the Big Ticket program, we would not have been able to participate due to staffing levels. STARS handled the program with aplomb.

Evaluation

In previous years, teens were required to write book reports to qualify for prizes. Prizes were awarded by drawing. From a survey that was taken in early 2001, the committee found that the teens preferred to be rewarded at levels of achievement, not by the number of books read. The concept of rewarding reading at the 200, 400, 600, and so on, page levels was instituted.

Another survey was conducted at the end of the 2001 summer reading program. The survey results allowed the librarians to tweak the successful 2001 program to produce an equally successful program in 2002. The 2002 summer reading program showed a 4.5 percent increase in participation over the previous year. More importantly, there was a 43 percent increase in the number of pages read—from 1,682,187 in 2001, to 2,408,761 in 2002. In the 2002 program, there was an increase of 35 percent in high school age registration, and a 69 percent increase of that age group in participation at the various levels. Although the number signing up in 2002 is not significantly higher than the 2001 levels, participation at the various reading plateaus increased sharply.

Impact of the Program

Getting Naperville's overscheduled young adult community involved in Naperville Public Library's summer reading program was a challenge that was hit head on in early 2001.

School visits were inaugurated for middle and high schools prior to the end of the school year. When the librarians went on the school visits, in addition to talking about the summer reading program they also announced the volunteer opportunities available at the library during the summer.

In anticipation of the summer reading program, the YA collection was enhanced by tracking materials popular with teens and providing additional copies of those materials. From comments made by young adults, the library greatly increased the graphic novel collection. Teen magazine circulation increased after additional copies of popular titles were ordered. On the Web site, a link just for teens was improved. Programming specifically for teens was scheduled. Emphasis was placed on supplementing what young adults were getting in school.

The visual aspects of the summer reading program were enhanced. Lively graphics were used on table toppers and bookmarks. The registration table was moved to a prominent position, and the number of decorations was increased. Local celebrities were honorees at the ending prize raffle. These changes in the program resulted in an increase of participation from 391 in 2000, to 2,064 in 2001 (456 percent), with a 40 percent increase in YA fiction circulation.

The Naperville Public Library's young adult summer reading program in still evolving. The 2003 program looks to be even bigger and better. A successful program was generated from what teens said they wanted. The young adults' participation as volunteers gives them ownership of the program, teaches commitment, enhances the joy of reading, and works as a great ego booster. The staff has found that supervising the teen volunteers increases interaction with the young adults and gives the teens a better idea of what is involved in working in a library and the duties of professional librarians.

For More Information

Becky Hollis
Naperville Public Library
2035 S. Naper Blvd.
Naperville, IL 60565
(630) 961-4100, ext. 2200
(630) 961-4119 (fax)
bhollis@lib.naperville.il.us

RELAX.READ Book Blitz

Mastics-Moriches-Shirley Community Library, Shirley, N.Y., and William Floyd High School Library, Mastic Beach, N.Y.

Target Audience

Senior high school students

Program Description

The RELAX.READ Book Blitz was a week-long campaign designed to promote recreational reading during

summer months. It was planned and implemented as a collaborative effort of the William Floyd High School Library and the teen services department of the Mastics-Moriches-Shirley Community Library. RELAX.READ was the theme for the community library's summer reading club. It was adopted as the theme for this event, which took place in the William Floyd High School Library during National Library Week, April 15–19, 2002. Throughout each day of the Blitz, English teachers brought their classes to the library to experience a variety of displays and presentations. Each class period included:

1. a brief introductory presentation by high school librarians on why summer reading is entertaining and beneficial;

2. booktalks by librarians and students;

3. genre book displays;

4. a community library booth with summer programming information, library card registration, promotional giveaways, and book raffles;

5. displays of suggested reading lists for ninth, tenth, eleventh, and twelfth grades;

6. a videotaped library rap performed by students;

7. a photo booth where students had Polaroid photos taken in our *RELAX.READ* beach setting;

8. a video booth where students earned special prizes if they videotaped a testimonial on books, reading, or their favorite librarian; and

9. displays of READ posters featuring teachers and administrators with their favorite books.

Sponsoring Institution

William Floyd Senior High School serves 2,769 students in ninth through twelfth grades. In September of 1999, the library moved into their six-thousand-square-foot, state-of-the-art facility featuring forty networked computers and seating for two hundred. In addition to integrating library resources and activities into the curriculum, the library's media center has maintained a strong emphasis on literature and reading. The University of the State of New York, State Education Department, designates it as an Electronic Doorway Library.

The teen services department of the Mastics-Moriches-Shirley Community Library serves five thousand district teens in seventh through twelfth grades. The 875-square-foot teen area has 9 computers and seating for 25. In fiscal year 2001–2002, more than 28,500 YA items were circulated.

The community library is committed to serving teenagers. In 2000, formal learning support and commons space were among the five service responses selected by the library's Planning for Results Committee. The objectives set forth for formal learning support for students in seventh through twelfth grades have already been met. These objectives include individualized homework help service on a weekly basis, review sessions for New York State Regents examinations, and annual PSAT and SAT review courses. The renovations to create a teen commons space in the library will be complete by mid-June 2003.

Young Adult Demographics

According to U.S. Census figures for 2000, the local adolescent population is 78.5 percent Caucasian, 12.4 percent Hispanic, 7.5 percent African-American, and 1.2 percent Asian. The median household income is $53,974, and 8.4 percent of district families have incomes below poverty level. The female population is slightly higher than the male population.

Program Participants

Book Blitz targeted ninth through twelfth graders in the William Floyd High School. Approximately 2,760 students attend the high school. It is the fourth largest school district in Suffolk County. Nearly 1,500 students attended the Book Blitz that week, as well as 30 teachers and staff. Most classes were ninth- through eleventh-grade students.

Youth Participation

Youth participation was the most exciting and effective component of the Book Blitz. Teens were invited to participate by school media specialists. Some of them developed testimonials for several books. Many of them added to their repertoires as the week progressed. Those of us who listened to them every day witnessed a growing sense of self-confidence as their expertise and delivery was perfected. Each of them had a remarkable way of getting a tough audience—their peers—to agree with them that reading is good and that these books were great reads. The students' preparation was done entirely on their own time.

The rappers, members of the varsity football team, wrote their own lyrics and recorded their performance after school.

Staff and Volunteers

Four full-time school media specialists and one full-time YA librarian devoted approximately fifteen to twenty staff hours to the planning of this event. The most time-intensive and challenging tasks were scheduling the class visits and coordinating the schedules of the twelve students who volunteered to present book testimonials. Throughout the week it was all hands on deck as school and public librarians were present for the event from 7:30 A.M. until the conclusion of the school day at 2 P.M. Four professional librarians logged a total 112 hours (28 hours each). The school's AV staff also spent about four hours videotaping the testimonials and the rappers.

Special guests, gratis of course, included school administrators, the community library director, and even the Suffolk County Library System YA specialist Tracey Firestone, an alumna of William Floyd High School, who graciously treated us to a few enticing booktalks.

Budget

The staff operating budgets of both the community library and William Floyd High School funded most of Book Blitz. Funding for this event, apart from staff time, was actually quite minimal. The community library purchased a Tiki hut kit for about $200. It was to be our beach setting for the Polaroid shots of teens reading. It turned out to be a dismal failure structurally, so we were partially refunded. Ultimately, the beach setting was created with a market umbrella ($50) and two portable canvas chairs ($15 each). Four grass skirts ($10 each) and four grass hats were also purchased ($2 each); the teens used them to dress up for the photos. The community library spent $450 on Polaroid film and $100 on paperbacks for raffles. Librarians themselves donated $300 for gift certificates from a local bookstore to show our appreciation to the students that gave book testimonials.

Evaluation

Although Book Blitz was not formally evaluated, several factors demonstrate the impact of the event. During the summer of 2002 community library circulation for young adult materials increased by 19 percent over circulation of the same material types during the summer of 2000. YA circulation for the summer of 2001 was not counted since a mandatory reading assignment for all secondary students was instituted that summer that may have accounted for a 21 percent increase in circulation of YA materials. The table below illustrates circu-

lation statistics.

	YA items circulated
Summer 2000	6,481
Summer 2001	8,205
Summer 2002	8,000

The second factor that demonstrates the impact of Book Blitz is the increase in summer reading club statistics. In the summer of 2001, 214 teens registered for the club and read a total of 543 books. In the summer of 2002, 303 teens registered and read a total of 733 books, even more than in 2001, when the district assigned mandatory summer reading.

All of the media specialists and community librarians were familiar with book titles discussed, displayed, and recommended at the event. Each library experienced an increased demand for these titles. All staff enjoyed informal chats with teens looking for books to read that summer. Media specialists occasionally visited the community library and talked with teens about the books and about Blitz. Also, the recommended reading lists created for Blitz continue to be a valuable resource to teens, librarians, teachers, and parents. It was a memorable way to celebrate National Library Week.

Impact of the Program

The RELAX.READ Book Blitz was an important program because it provided a rare opportunity to bring teens and books together in a relaxed and festive setting. The displays and activities were designed to expose students to a vast number of outstanding books, both old and new. The school/public library partnership was emphasized to reinforce the concept that both agencies not only serve the same population, but that their services are integrated and would continue seamlessly throughout the year. The opportunity for the community library to promote the RELAX.READ summer reading program to a large, captive audience and to register teens for library cards was unprecedented. But the student testimonials about the books they had read and enjoyed were by far the most dramatic vehicle to entice teens to read. They were honest, passionate, funny, and always captivating. From Dickens' *Great Expectations* to Benchley's *Jaws* to Chopin's *The Awakening*, the message was that reading is cool, cool kids read, and there are some great stories out there that are just too good to miss. Some students even took the opportunity to plug librarians as influential reading advisors. Nobody said it better than the teens themselves.

For More Information

Teri Germano
Mastics-Moriches-Shirley Community Library
Shirley, NY 11967
(631) 399-1511, ext. 254
(631)281-4442 (fax)
tgermano@suffolk.lib.ny.us

Teen2Teen: Book Recommendations by Teens4Teens

Montgomery County Public Libraries, Rockville, Maryland

Target Audience

Middle, junior high, and senior high school students as well as at-risk and special-needs teens

Program Description

Capitalizing on the growing success of the summer reading program for children, Montgomery County Public Libraries (MCPL) started a similar program for teens in 2001. Teens (grades seven through twelve) participate by writing short recommendations of recently read books. Approximately 100 recommendations were chosen for compilation into a booklet titled *Teen2Teen*: Book Recommendations by Teens4Teens. The booklet,

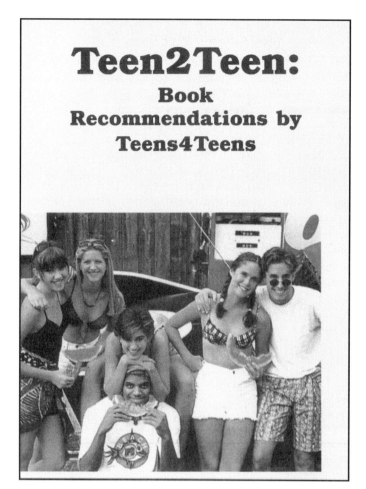

Teen2Teen: Book Recommendations by Teens4Teens

funded by the Friends of the Library, is distributed throughout the library system during Teen Read Week, and is used in school visits and by teens and parents as a source of reading suggestions throughout the year. Where applicable, the bibliographic information includes whether the title is owned as a sound recording, in large-type format, and in other languages. To make it easier to find books by categories, there is a listing of the titles by genre. In addition, *Teen2Teen* is posted on the library's teen Web page, and teens can submit recommendations online.

Sponsoring Institution

MCPL serves a fast-growing and diverse community that is part of the Washington, D.C., metropolitan area. Approximately 900,000 people live in the county; more than 98,000 are between the ages of ten and seventeen. The county has both great wealth and many residents needing government assistance. The library system strives to meet the considerable range of needs with a variety of formats, more than 2.5 million materials, 452 computers available to the public, a large number of databases in many subjects, a Web site tailored to community interests, and 24-hour reference (as part of a consortium) and renewal services as well as programs for all ages both within the libraries and out in the communities.

Young Adult Demographics

One out of every nine county residents is between ages eleven and eighteen. The teen population is very diverse, with more than 161 countries represented in the public school system. This system is the largest in Maryland, the nineteenth largest in the country, and the twelfth fastest growing in the country. The schools are highly competitive (in the June 2, 2003, issue of *Newsweek*, five of the county's twenty-three high schools are listed among the nation's hundred top public schools.) Ninety percent of the public school students graduate, and 64 percent take honors and advanced placement classes. Despite being one of the wealthiest counties, more than one-fifth of the students receive food and nutritional assistance, and more than one-third have received such assistance at some time during their school years. Many county teens attend the numerous private schools in the county, and there is a growing number of home-schooled teens. Teens have a wide variety of academic and recreational activities to choose from, and many work at part-time jobs and volunteer in the community.

Program Participants

The *Teen2Teen* booklet is by and for Montgomery County teens, ages eleven to eighteen. Participation by teens in the summer reading club has increased in the two years the program has existed. In 2001, ten libraries participated and more than three hundred teens joined the club and provided recommendations. The following year, fourteen libraries participated, and entries could also be submitted online, allowing teens to continue to be part of the program while they were on vacation. More than four hundred teens joined the program and submitted recommendations.

Youth Participation

Encouraging participation by teens in the summer reading program is the library system's goal. Teens take part in the program by submitting (in writing or online) short recommendations (two to three sentences) of recently read books. For each of the two issues printed (2001, 2002), a group of librarians compiled approximately one hundred recommendations from the more than four hundred submitted, and added a list of the titles by genre. The booklet, which comes out during Teen Read Week, is a tangible result of this teen participation and an attractive way of promoting reading (and a little writing), with title suggestions from fellow teens. This year the booklet will sport a teen-designed cover.

Staff and Volunteers

Each participating library has one librarian or library associate who briefly checks that library's submissions for readability and then sends them to a member of the

compilation group. That group has four members (librarians or library associates) who select the titles, ensuring a large variety of reading interests and reading levels and a geographical cross-section of teens around the county. The compilation group adds bibliographic information for each title and also gets all the material camera-ready on disk. Another librarian coordinates the booklet project through the printing and distribution processes, and the webmistress posts the booklet.

Budget

Teen2Teen is funded by the Friends of the Library, Montgomery County, Inc., which provides $1,500, covering all printing costs of the booklet. Staff members work on this project during their regularly scheduled times; when extra hours are needed, they are paid with library substitute funds. Each participating library's staff member spends between one and two hours on this project, and members of the compilation group each work about ten hours.

Evaluation

Feedback from the first year's recommendations led to a few adaptations on the form used last year; for example, encouraging more description of the book and less opinion. While no formal evaluation of the booklet has taken place, the scarcity of copies and teens asking for listed books while holding a booklet in their hands attest to its popularity. The teen Web page has a form for teens to recommend books all year round for periodic posting on the site.

Impact of the Program

Teens write all the recommendations of the books they have chosen to read. The teens look forward to seeing themselves in print and, of course, prefer to get their reading suggestions from peers. Teens with special needs benefit from the bibliographic information that includes whether a book comes in large-type format, as a sound recording, and in other languages.

Parents and teachers use the booklet to encourage their teens' reading and keep current in young adult reading interests. Librarians use *Teen2Teen* for title suggestions for the public and themselves (particularly good for non-YA librarians) and for promoting teen library services while visiting schools and out in the communities.

All Montgomery County teens have access to *Teen2Teen* through distribution in the public libraries and schools and the booklet's posting on the library's teen Web page. Five thousand copies were printed in 2001, and six thousand were printed for the 2002 issue. The booklet has become the library system's official middle school summer reading list.

It has been fascinating to see the increasing interest in the program, the breadth of reading tastes, and the speed with which new titles gain a foothold among teens as well as the enduring power of some classics.

For More Information

Susan H. Levine
Silver Spring Library
8901 Colesville Rd.
Silver Spring, MD 20910
(301) 565-7689
(301) 565-7301 (fax)
susan.levine@montgomerycountymd.gov

Teen Productions

Flint (Mich.) Public Library

Target Audience

Middle, junior high, and senior high school students

Program Description

Teen Productions was the library's alternative to a summer reading club for teens. It consisted of a series of three-day creative workshops that allowed teens to develop their own themes and ideas:

- **Write Stuff workshop:** Poet and staff librarian Renee Nixon led a teen workshop on developing ideas and getting them down on paper.

- **Cartooning workshop**: Local art teacher and cartoonist John Sheathelm joined teens in a workshop to give advice on drawing and developing creative creatures.

- **Digital photography workshop:** Teens learned how the digital camera works, then, using the library's camera (or their own), they photographed images around the library. Finally, they came back to the lab to download, adjust, and print the images out.

- **Bookmaking workshop:** Teens designed and constructed books for pleasure and personal use. They learned to make paper, several simple books, paper cutting, and origami.

- **Puppetry workshop**: Puppet master and Flint Public Library (FPL) staff member Brenda Harris taught puppet construction, basic movements, and voice techniques as this class prepared for a performance as a finale on the last Saturday of the program.

- **Web page Authoring workshop**: Local Flint webmistress Erica Olsen taught teens the secrets of writing fabulous Web pages.

A gala exhibit of all the creative products was held at the end of the summer. Later teens would share what they had learned by either giving a program at the library or teaching others what they had learned in their various workshops. This then would generate programming for teens driven by teen interest and expertise.

Sponsoring Institution

Serving an urban, underserved population of 124,943 residents (according to the 2000 Census), FPL is a mid-sized library system in Michigan. It has a centrally located main library, three branches, and a bookmobile. The main library is a central resource in the City of Flint and Genesee County (pop. 436,141) for research and information, and it is visited everyday by citizens of all ages. The facility is located centrally in Flint's Cultural Center. As an ideal focal point for citywide teen programming, it is also strategically located next to Flint Central High School, Whittier Middle School, and Sarvis-Pierce Elementary School and easily accessible via the citywide bus system.

Young Adult Demographics

- Flint teens numbered more than 64,800 in the 2000 Census.

- 19 percent live in child poverty (ranking Genesee Co. 73 of 83 counties in Michigan).

- 37.1 percent of teens receive free/reduced school lunches.

- The teen pregnancy rate is 33.2/1000 (rank 75/81).

- The high school dropout rate is 4.1 percent (rank 44/80).

(Source: *Kids Count in Michigan 2002 Data Book* [Michigan League of Human Services, 2000])

Genesee County is a community where child poverty in ages eleven through nineteen has increased by 13 percent and ranks seventy-eighth out of eighty-three counties. Thirty-seven percent more children are receiving free or reduced-price school lunches in 1999 than 1990. Abuse or neglect cases have risen by 204 percent over a ten-year period, and the unemployment rate is 11.6 percent in the City of Flint. Forty-six percent of the total births in Genesee County in 1998 were "non-marital," which ranks 64 out of 70 counties rated in Michigan.

The above figures, taken from the *Kids Count in Michigan 2002 Data Book*, underscore the importance of taking the library programs into the community to reach teens who are in stressful family situations and are not likely to participate in positive reading activities on a regular basis, if at all.

Program Participants

Aproximately 125 teens participated in the program. Attendance at each workshop varied according to complexity and availability of space.

Later, teens shared their expertise gained through the workshops with more than two hundred other library patrons throughout the summer and school year. Participants presented puppet shows, instructed other teens on Web page design and authoring, and used digital cameras to record library programming throughout the year and for our Teen Source Web page program documentation.

Youth Participation

Workshop topics were chosen based upon input from teens who participated in library activities during the school year. Young adult services offers programming throughout the year and also has a regular Tuesday Open Lab where teens can spend time in the Internet training lab, receiving help from the cybrarian and young adult services librarian.

Teens who had expertise were recruited to help instruct others in the workshops. Youth sharing their skills with their peers was a part of the program.

Teens also shared the experience gained in the workshops with other library patrons by developing a

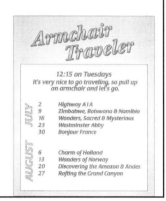
library program, helping to design the library's young adult Web site, or by documenting a library activity during the school year.

Staff and Volunteers

There were two staff members involved in the planning and implementation of the programs: the young adult librarian and the supervisor of services to children and young teens. Three other staff members taught several workshops: bookmaking, puppetry, and digital cameras. Two outside experts were also hired to teach classes in cartooning and Web authoring.

Budget

The Teen Production workshops were paid for by FPL. Partial funding was secured from the Friends of the Flint Public Library. Staff were recruited to present programs whenever possible in order to curb costs.

Two outside expert workshop leaders (three classes/three hours each, $300)	$600
Supplies and misc.	$300
Total	**$900**

Evaluation

At the end of each class a mini-survey was distributed. Staff also collected word-of-mouth comments. Feedback from parents or guardians was documented, and recommendations from teens were considered when planning the following year's workshops.

Impact of the Program

Teens love technology! Teens are also very creative. Many teens see themselves as writers, artists, or creators of products. What is often lacking is the opportunity to explore this creativity due to a lack of resources or adequate instruction.

When a community entity such as the library can pull together the teens, the resources, and the instructors, the creative products emerge without end. All of the classes were full and well attended. The response from teens, their parents, and the community was so positive that the program will be repeated this summer.

Many teens have provided feedback on how their interest in technology has evolved from a hobby to a career pathway. This adds value to the community-at-large as well as to the teens on a personal level.

Teens have returned to share their skills by providing content and helping to design the Teen Source young adult Web pages. They have also expressed pride at the new status they enjoy in their families as computer experts.

Young adults now see the library as a valuable and viable resource. Libraries enrich their lives in meaningful ways.

For More Information

Leslie A. Acevedo
Young Adult Services Librarian
Flint Public Library
1026 E. Kearsley St.
Flint, MI 48502
(810) 232-7111
(810) 249-2633 (fax)
lacevedo@flint.lib.mi.us

Xtreme

Pikes Peak Library District, Colorado Springs, Colo.

Target Audience

Middle, junior high, and senior high school students

Program Description

During summer 2002, the Pikes Peak Library District (PPLD) offered a young adult summer reading program titled Xtreme. Teens collected Xtreme character trading cards (for each book read, participants earned one trad-

ing card). Eighteen trading cards were available, but participants were only asked to read ten books and do ten activities to finish the game. Each card included a choice of activities and factoids related to the subject. Activities and books earned chances in the weekly prize drawings, and specific prizes were offered as incremental incentives. Additional books earned additional trading cards. Each finisher won a t-shirt and an invitation to a free showing of the X-Games IMAX film, *Ultimate X*. A special prize was given for reading the All Pikes Peak Read selection, *To Kill a Mockingbird*. For the first time, PPLD also offered four special YA programs. Nearly three thousand young adults participated in Xtreme.

Sponsoring Institution

PPLD is a dynamic public library system serving one of the fastest growing populations in Colorado (approximately 490,000). In 2002, the library district served more than 2.6 million visitors; circulated 5.2 million items; provided programs in arts and education for 220,000 children, teens, and adults; and reached thousands of residents through cablecasts on Adelphia cable channel 17. The library is tax-supported and funded as a special district, but it also receives funding from specific ownership taxes, fines and fees, interest earnings, gifts, and private fundraising efforts. Its mission is "to provide resources and service to inform, empower, inspire and encourage respect for individuals and ideas." PPLD was one of the first libraries in Colorado to encourage a proactive, visible, and well-integrated young adult team as part of its adult services staff. The team coordinates booktalks in local schools, plans teen programming, and works with a youth advisory council; it also spearheaded a statewide collaboration effort with other Colorado library young adult advocates.

Young Adult Demographics

Young adults make up approximately 13 percent of the population in El Paso County, which encompasses PPLD. The district is predominantly Caucasian (81 percent), with an Hispanic population of about 12 percent. African-Americans in the county number 6 percent, and Asians, 2.9 percent. The high school graduation rate in El Paso County is 83 percent, although that of the largest school district served by the library is only 72.5 percent. In the 2000 Colorado Scholastic Assessment Program (CSAP) Reading Assessment Tests, the percentage of seventh graders deemed proficient or advanced in El Paso County schools ranged from a low of 50 percent to a high of 87 percent (state average was 62 percent). The young adult team at PPLD concentrates its summer reading efforts on the forgotten middle school-aged student, hoping, among other things, to work with the community to improve literacy and high school graduation rates.

The following bookmarks are shown in the image:

X-TREME COURAGE
- McKinley, Robin — The Hero and the C...
- McKinley, Robin — The Outlaws of Sh...
- Michaelson, Ben — Touching Spirit B...
- Myers, Walter D... — Fallen Angels
- Nielsen, Jerri -...
- Pinkney, Andre... — Let It Shine: S... Women Freed...
- Read, Piers... — Alive
- Rottman, S...
- Schwager, ... — Gutsy Girls
- Ten Boom... — The Hidin...
- Whelan, ... — Homeles...
- Wolff, V... — True Be...
- Crea... Libra...

X-TREMELY ATHLETIC
- Lee, Marie G. — Necessary Rou...
- Levy, Marilyn — Run for Your L...
- Miller, Marla — All American ...
- Myers, Walter... — Slam!
- Powell, Rand... — Run if You D...
- Rottman, S. — Head Above...
- Ryan, Joan — Little Girls in...
- Sweeney, J... — Players
- Wells, Ros... — When No ...
- Wolff, Virg... — Bat 6
- Crea... County... Color... Advoc... S... www...

X-TREMELY IMAGINATIVE
- Jones, Diana Wynne — Howl's Moving Castle
- Juster, Norton — Phantom Tollbooth
- Kindl, Patrice - Owl...
- King, J. Robert - M...
- Murphey, Rita — Night Flying
- Nix, Garth - Sab...
- Pierce, Meredit... — Treasure at the Tanglewood
- Pullman, Phili... — Golden Comp...
- Springer, Na... — I am Mordre...
- Stewart, Se... — Nobody's S...
- Thompson,...
- Tolkien, J...
- Wrede,... — Talking ...
- Create... Library... Summ... www...

X-TREMELY SAD
- Kjelgaard, Jim - Big Red
- McDaniel, Lurlene — To Live Again
- McDonald, Joyce — Swallowing Stones
- Rawlings, Marjorie - Yearling
- Rawls, Wilson — Where the Red Fern Grows
- Ruby, Lois - Miriam's Well
- Segal, Eric - Love Story
- Tomlinson, Theresa — Dancing Through the Shadows
- Trueman, Terry — Stuck in Neutral
- Voigt, Cynthia — Izzy Willy Nilly
- Woodson, Jacqueline — If You Come Softly
- Wunderli, Stephen — Heartbeat of Halftime
- Created by Pikes Peak Library District for Colorado Young Adult Advocate in Libraries, Summer 2002 www.aclin.org/~cyaal/

Program Participants

The young adult summer reading program was designed for young adults in grades six through twelve (ages eleven through eighteen). The vast majority of registrants for the program were in middle school (age eleven through fourteen), but children as young as nine and as old as eighteen participated. The young adult team marketed the program in middle schools and to fifth graders in all the local school districts, and in teen venues throughout the city.

Officially, 2,889 students participated in Xtreme in 2002. Of those, 903 finished the program, having read at least ten books and completed at least ten of the suggested activities. PPLD set the bar extremely high by requiring the teens to read ten books, and the participants rose to the occasion, increasing by nearly 40 percent the number of finishers from the previous year. Without lowering expectations, PPLD has seen the number of teens participating in summer reading programs grow significantly over the past few years.

Youth Participation

Xtreme 2002 built on the popularity of character trading cards with young adults to create a unique summer reading program. Extensive young adult input insured that the cards created for the program would have as much appeal as the t-shirts and IMAX passes that were awarded to students who completed the summer reading program. The YA team worked most closely with the twenty-member youth advisory council, teens who were involved from conception to completion of the program. The teens assisted staff in many ways: choosing the appropriate artwork and character names for the trading cards; planning and supporting the four programs offered during the summer; promoting the program in their schools and among their friends; writing a rap up at the end of the summer that was performed by staff at the August Colorado Young Adult Advocates in Libraries (C'YAAL) summer reading "rap" up session; counting out prizes to be distributed to branches; and making suggestions for improvements in future summer reading programs (such as how to involve older teens, how to make the game more challenging, program suggestions).

Staff and Volunteers

The eight members of the young adult team (three librarians and five information technicians) were the most heavily involved in planning, administering, and evaluating the summer reading program. Individual tasks were divided up based on expertise and interest, but everyone was deeply involved in the early creative phase when the program began to take shape. The YA team also worked collaboratively with youth advocates from other libraries throughout the state in creating the text of the trading cards and bookmarks, in securing the graphic artist, in printing and distributing the trading cards, and brainstorming programming ideas. Also, each local branch had a YA liaison who worked closely with the YA team to help the program run smoothly. During the game all public services staff throughout the district were involved in the program, since they promoted the game and teens collected their prizes at the reference desks. Staff was encouraged to buy an Xtreme t-shirt as a summer reading fundraiser, wear the shirt to advertise the program, and become knowledgeable about the game. PPLD purposely built in this youth-staff contact to help build a positive relationship between the teens and the adults who served them.

Budget

The YA team had an $8,600 budget in 2002, much of which was earmarked for the summer reading program.

The largest expense was for t-shirts ($4,500). PPLD also contributed $250 toward the $500 paid the graphic artist, and paid $1,250 for the printing of the Xtreme trading cards. Other programming expenses included $500 for summer programs (food and speakers) and $500 for the IMAX party. Promotional materials, game cards, bookmarks, and other printed materials were produced in-house by the PPLD print shop and were not charged separately to the YA team budget. Preparation and administrative costs are considered part of the YA team's regular duties as teen advocates in the library and were not charged as separate expense items. Local sponsors who partnered with the library to promote the young adult summer reading program donated most prizes. Sponsors included Pepsi, Chipotle, Wendy's, Nickel-a-Play, Cinemark/IMAX Theater, Chick-fil-A, Sky Sox, Mountasia, Six Flags, Royal Gorge, Colorado Springs Parks and Recreation—Aquatics and Sertich Ice Center, Harmony Bowl, Champions Golf and Games, Skate City, local malls, Papa John's Pizza, Extreme Pizza, and Pikes Peak International Raceway. The value of coupons, gift certificates, and discounts from these sponsors totaled in excess of $30,000.

Evaluation

Year of program	# of participants	# of finishers
1999	1,367	536
2000	1,827	568
2001	2,571	647
2002	2,889	903

The numbers speak for themselves, but are only part of the evaluation process. Participants in the 2002 summer reading program increased 111 percent over 1999, 58 percent over 2000, and 12.4 percent over 2001. Even more impressive are the numbers of finishers (ten books/ten activities). The 903 finishers in 2002 represented a whopping 39.5 percent increase over 2001, a 59 percent increase over 2000, and a 68 percent increase over 1999. The popular trading cards were an important reason for the high numbers of finishers in 2002, but branch staff worked hard to promote the program in schools and market the program in their branches, contributing to its success. Branch liaisons trained their staff well and built strong relationships with schools, families, and youth. After looking at the numbers and congratulating themselves for the increases, the YA team then set out to use what it had learned from their 2002 experiences to create an even better program in 2003. They turned first to the youth advisory council. The teens suggested a number of ideas that have been incorporated into Fourteeners, the 2003 program: discussion groups to pull in older teens; options for harder activities and books to challenge better readers without discouraging struggling readers; better prizes; and incentives to read beyond the required ten books. (The 2003 program has incorporated a Beyond Fourteeners component, in which money will be donated to a local charity for every book read beyond the required ten.) The teens have also been more involved in planning activities and making suggestions for program content.

The YA team also sought branch feedback, the result of which has been the development of an online registration process, streamlining of record keeping (more responsibility on the shoulders of the youth themselves), and elimination of weekly prize drawings (replaced by better general prizes and drawings at programs). Finally, a number of schools, at the library's urging, have become more active in promoting the teen summer reading program, recognizing the advantages it offers to their students and teachers. Many of these changes grew out of the evaluation of the 2002 program, examining both its successes and its shortcomings.

Impact of the Program

A well-thought-out young adult summer reading program is important to those who participate, to their families, and to the community at large for a variety of reasons tied to the developmental needs of teens. First is its impact on academic success and support of statewide educational goals. Research shows that students participating in a summer reading program are more likely to read at or above their grade level than nonparticipating peers, and are more likely to retain those skills during the subsequent school year. Moreover, youth who do a lot of voluntary reading have been shown to develop positive attitudes toward reading in general. This is no less true for teenagers than for younger children. Obviously, the PPLD young adult summer reading program had an important literacy component, providing youth with that all-important reading for pleasure. But it had a much broader purpose, as well.

For instance, Xtreme was helpful in strengthening relationships. It promoted a sense of community among teenagers by giving them an opportunity to connect with other teens in a positive environment. Programs and activities linked kids with other kids, which was especially important for the many home-schoolers who participated in the program. In addition, many activities encouraged family involvement, thereby supporting and enhancing parent and teen relationships in a unique and fun way. Finally, the game encouraged teens to develop a positive interaction with adults outside their families, fostering a sense of respect from the community at large.

Teens need and deserve respect. Collaborating with the library, community businesses and organizations supported and recognized the significant efforts of the teens. The business community showed teens that they cared about their welfare and their future by donating thousands of dollars worth of free merchandise as prizes and incentives. Through its sponsors, therefore, Xtreme provided a forum in which the community could show its support for teens by providing food and wholesome teen activities, activities that were positive, safe, and fun to do. In addition, Xtreme was designed to respect the participants' rights to choose their own reading material, with the understanding that reading ability and interests varied widely. The reading lists distributed as part of the program also reflected the diverse interests of young adults and the activities gave the participants many options from which to choose.

Finally, collaboration was an important component of the summer reading program. Adults collaborated with teens throughout the process. Through C'YAAL, librarians from PPLD collaborated with librarians from around the state to plan and execute the program. The library collaborated with local merchants and organizations by soliciting their sponsorship of Xtreme. Local school districts collaborated with the library to advertise, encourage, and reward participation in the program, and the YA team collaborated with branch staff to administer an integrated summer reading program throughout the entire district. As a result, branch participation in and advocacy of teen programs and involvement have increased tremendously.

For More Information

Vickie Pasicznyuk
Bonnie Phinney
Pikes Peak Library District
5550 N. Union Blvd.
Colorado Springs, CO 80918
(719) 531-6333. ext. 1412/1207
(719) 528-5289 (fax)
vpasicznyuk@ppld.org
bphinney@ppld.org

8. Teen Advisory Boards

One of the best and easiest ways of meeting the needs of young adults in libraries is to create an advisory board of teens to provide input into these services. The Coshocton Public Library teen advisory board is an excellent example of a traditional board. Its members plan programs for library users of all ages, assist with planning the young adult summer reading program, provide input on collection development decisions, and volunteer on various library projects. Dayton Metro Library's Japanese anime advisory board provides a more specific function of assisting with the collection development of anime films and graphic novels. This group was founded by a librarian who observed young adult interest in sketching anime characters in the library. Both advisory boards have provided input that resulted in an increase in young adult circulation in their respective libraries.

Coshocton Public Library Teen Advisory Board

Coshocton (Ohio) Public Library

Target Audience

Middle, junior high, and senior high school students

Program Description

Established in 1996, the Coshocton Public Library (CPL) teen advisory board invites teens in seventh through twelfth grades to participate in monthly meetings, program planning and implementation, and materials selection for the young adult collection. The teens have performed reader's theater productions, completed volunteer activities that would have taken staff many hours to finish, created and manned games for children's programs, published bookmarks and newsletters, and have gone on shopping field trips

together. They have been helpful in creating enjoyable, entertaining, and educational programs for all ages at the library. Many of their activities have been featured on the See YA Around Web site (www.cplrmh.com) and in the book, *101+ Teen Programs That Work* (Neal-Schuman, 2002) by RoseMary Honnold, the group's advisor. Their Monopoly tournament was featured in a Nickelodeon spot called "In Play Today" in June 2002.

Sponsoring Institution

CPL serves Coshocton County, a rural community in east central Ohio. The library serves a population of more than 36,000 with a main library, a branch, and a bookmobile. Under the direction of Ann Miller, the library's collection numbers 129,044 items, with a circulation of 529,429 items for 2002, ranking 66 out of 250 Ohio libraries. Young adult services were established when C. Allen Nichols spoke to the staff at an in-service program. Four staff members were inspired to use their spare time to build a teen advisory board to develop programming and expand the young adult collection. When the group proved itself to be successful, a new position was created on the staff for a young adult services coordinator. More programs and annual events for teens have become part of the library calendar because of teen advisory board efforts.

Young Adult Demographics

According to the Coshocton County Profile for 2003, there are approximately 4,224 teens between the ages of twelve and nineteen. Approximately 2,015 are female and 2,209 are male. The high school graduation rate for the county is 81.7 percent. There are three high schools and one vocational school in the county as well as a number of home-schooled students.

Program Participants

While the teen advisory board is designed for teens aged twelve through nineteen, or grades seven through twelve, the benefits of their work have been enjoyed by patrons of all ages. Children, teens, and adults have enjoyed bigger and better programs as a result of the board's efforts, and the teens have a better collection and a more comfortable room to enjoy.

Over the seven years the teen advisory board has operated, there have been twelve to twenty-two members participating each year. These teens have reached many other teens through the programs they have put together. Siblings and friends of members have joined the group. Summer reading programs that the teens help develop draw about 120 participants each summer. Social programs average twenty to twenty-five teens each and occur about five to six times a year. As many as six independent games and drawings per year in the young adult room usually attract seventy-five to one hundred participants. All of these participants are in the target age group of twelve to nineteen years of age.

Youth Participation

Teen advisory board members are free to give feedback at the meeting following each program. They also fill out evaluations at the end of each year about the programs offered and about the board. The meetings are informal discussions and brainstorming sessions when planning programs, with every idea considered if not necessarily acted upon. The group has been flexible to adapt to the personality of new members each year. Some years the group has enjoyed writing, editing, and publishing a newsletter, other years the teens preferred working with younger children. Some teens prefer selecting books, magazines, and music for the collection. The Role-Playing Club, a spin-off group from the board, suggests role-playing and fantasy materials for the YA collection. The teen advisory board prepares craft materials for the children's department, decorates a holiday tree to represent the library for a community festival, and wraps gifts for homebound patrons. The Book Tree, built by the board in 2001, can be seen in the January 2002 issue of *American Libraries*. The role of the board in our library is flexible, but always helpful and productive.

Staff and Volunteers

One advisor oversees the group with another staff member assisting at the meetings when special projects need more guidance. The teens themselves are the volunteers involved in most of the programming and volunteer tasks.

Budget

The Friends of the Coshocton Public Library provides the funding for the teen advisory board. Our expenses include refreshments for the meetings and expenses for the book shopping trips. The refreshment budget is about $200 per year. The book trip budget is about $400 per trip. The board is treated to a lunch, and the rest goes to book purchases. In exchange, the board helps set up and tear down the annual big book sale sponsored by the Friends of the Library. Small gifts and treats are given to the teens when available from Naeir.org to thank them for their work. The Friends of the Library operates a book store at the library three days a week to raise funds for programming and other equipment that can't find its way into the library's budget. The teens can focus on doing volunteer work and creating programs rather than trying to raise money.

Evaluation

Collection development in the young adult area has been greatly improved since the establishment of the teen advisory board. More and different magazines and additions of graphic novels, CDs, and software to the collection have increased the size and variety of the collection and its circulation. Each meeting begins with a book discussion of what everyone has been reading and a quick look at what's new. The board has improved the environment of the YA room by suggesting the type of furniture to add and selecting posters for the walls. Their suggestions and interests have helped develop sections of the collection, and the shopping trips have been a valuable means of having their direct input. Their suggestions and participation have made the library a more welcoming and accommodating place for the teens in Coshocton County.

The experiences of the teen advisory board have benefited many other teens across the country through the librarians who have visited the See YA Around Web site and read *101+ Teen Programs That Work,* two popular works among young adult librarians that would not exist without the success of CPL's teen advisory board.

Impact of the Program

Several teens who joined the board in junior high have continued with the group until they graduated high school. A number of the Search Institute's (www.search-institute.org) forty developmental assets that teens need to become well-adjusted adults can be built by participating in a group like the teen advisory board. Interaction with another adult in a library who cares about the teens shows teens that they are valued by the community. Productive meetings and volunteer activities provide teens with an avenue to be creative, experience positive peer pressure, and develop positive values. Planning, accepting responsibility, and learning to work together helps the teens to be more socially competent and find a place where they belong and can contribute. When they see other teens read the books they've chosen, come to programs they've designed, see children having fun at events they are helping host, and hear audiences laugh or applaud at their antics at reader's theater or poetry readings, these teens feel a sense of purpose that builds their self esteem. At least one teen, Mamie A., enjoyed her experiences on the board and at the library so much that she is now in college to become a librarian.

For More Information

RoseMary Honnold
Coshocton Public Library
655 Main St.
Coshocton, OH 43812
(740) 622-0956, ext. 14
(740) 622-4331
honnolro@oplin.org

Japanese Anime Advisory Board

Dayton Metro Library, Kettering-Moraine Branch, Kettering, Ohio

Target Audience

Middle, junior high, and senior high school students

Program Description

Dayton Metro Library's (DML) Japanese anime advisory board was formed in November 2002. It is a forum for young adults to provide useful input on an art form that is rather misunderstood, but growing in popularity. The board consists of seven to fifteen members who meet monthly to screen and discuss a Japanese anime movie that is not owned by DML. After the screening, their comments are summarized and passed along to the person who orders the AV materials for the library. The group also plans additional anime-related activities throughout the year, such as movie marathons, sketching sessions, and workshops on how to create your own comic book. The Japanese anime advisory board functions as a teen voice for the system's selection of anime movies.

Sponsoring Institution

Kettering, Ohio, located five miles south of Dayton, is the seat of Montgomery County and principle city of the Miami Valley region. The library is frequented by middle and high school students during after-school hours. Getting young adults to attend programs at the library, however, has been a struggle until now.

The Kettering-Moraine branch library opened in March 1958, adjacent to Fairmont High School on land donated by the Kettering Board of Education. The building was expanded in 1966 and again in 1996. Kettering-Moraine is one of twenty-one locations in the DML system, and remains among those with the highest circulation in the system. In March 2003, Kettering-Moraine's YA circulation accounted for 3.75 percent of the total YA circulation. In the same month, Kettering-Moraine's DVD circulation accounted for 3.86 percent of the total DVD circulation for the system.

Young Adult Demographics

According to the 2000 U.S. Census, the city of Kettering, Ohio, has a total population of 57,502. The number of individuals between the ages of ten and nineteen amounts to 6,886, roughly 12 percent of the whole. The racial composition is as follows: 95.2 percent Caucasian, 1.7 percent African-American, and 1.4 percent Asian. The remaining 1.7 percent consists of those who are Native Hawaiian, Hispanic, or Latino, or of two or more races. Kettering's median household income in 1999 was $45,051. The median family income is $55,849; 4.1 percent of the families living in Kettering were listed as earning less than $15,000. Of the total number of households (25,657), 19.4 percent (4,977) are married couple families with children under eighteen. Households with a single female householder with children under eighteen make up 5.9 percent of the whole (1,501).

Program Participants

The idea for the Japanese anime advisory board evolved from observing middle school students sketching anime characters in the library. They often had book covers and notebooks covered with sketches of different characters. Japanese anime tends to attract kids who are not the superstars in school. They aren't usually jocks or involved in ten million extracurricular activities. These kids live vicariously through anime stories, whose characters often have superpowers and fantasy lives. The first Japanese anime advisory board meeting had eleven participants, ranging in age from eleven to eighteen. Ten out of the eleven were boys. The group has met six times now, and the members are quite different. The group now consists of eight girls and six boys ranging in age from eleven through seventeen.

Meeting attendance varies between six and eighteen teens. The best thing about this program is that it brings kids into the Kettering-Moraine branch library who would not normally come. One of the regulars now comes to the library every day after school. His anime artwork is part of a temporary exhibit of twenty-five pieces of Japanese anime advisory board anime drawings on display in the library's meeting room. This program has made the librarian more trusted and well known among the high school and middle school students, even the ones who aren't Japanese anime fans. Local teens now view the library in a more favorable light.

Youth Participation

This program would not exist without the young adults who participate. They pick the movies. They offer comments on the movies that are turned into thoughtful reviews. They help to set up and clean up after the meetings. They bring in new members. They plan additional activities. Finally, they offer comments on the benefit of such a program on their lives.

Staff and Volunteers

Only one DML reference librarian is involved in this program (unless you count the training specialist and training assistant, who supply the equipment for the movie screenings). The majority of the work is done by the most active members in the group. There are about five students that help set up for the meetings, get the movies, and clean up afterwards. One of the members usually helps with the refreshments by bringing in a bag of chips or pop. These kids also help in spreading the word in their schools and among their friends.

Budget

The program is mostly funded by DML. The teens contribute their time and occasional refreshments.

In-house costs include seventy-two staff hours per year at $14.70 per hour, or $1,058.40. Publicity costs run $150. A Proxima digital projector owned by the training office is loaned free of charge to branches for classes and programs; its approximate value is $2,700. The program costs include twelve DVDs screened per year at an average cost of $15 per movie (part rental/part purchase) for a total of $180; refreshments add another $78. Friends of the Library costs include $70 for a DVD player. Computer speakers were donated by a staff member. Overall, the program costs $1,536.40.

Evaluation

The Japanese anime advisory board has been in existence since October 2002. Since then, total YA circulation has risen by 22.3 percent (376 in October 2002 to 460 in April 2003). Since January 2002, YA circulation has risen 33.6 percent (306 in January 2002 to 460 in April 2003). The addition of Japanese manga to the YA collection, an expansion in the number of graphic novels, and an increase in YA programming have most likely contributed to this increase. This increase in circulation of YA materials, in addition to the evaluative comments provided by Japanese anime advisory board members, proves that this is a worthwhile program that should be continued.

Impact of the Program

As stated above, Japanese anime is a medium that that attracts a variety of kids. The kids who get the most out of anime are usually the artsy types, or loners who do not have throngs of friends. They do not typically participate in several extracurricular sports and clubs. However, they are often intelligent, creative, and looking for a way to meet other kids who share their interests.

Providing library programming that validates the significance of Japanese anime sends the message to these young adults that the library is interested in them. This creates a domino effect, and the message spreads to other students in the school and in the community.

For More Information

Victoria Vogel
Dayton Metro Library
Kettering-Moraine Branch
3496 Far Hills Ave.
Kettering, OH 45429
(937) 227-9509
(937) 298-6114 (fax)
km_victoria@dayton.lib.oh.us

9. Young Adults with Disabilities

Young adults with multiple disabilities are often overlooked in library programs and services. The two programs featured in this chapter address the needs of this population by providing stories and reader's advisory services to public school groups in the public library. Library Services for Teens with Special Needs designed its own unique curriculum to address the needs of students with multiple disabilities, while Teen Time Special was able to adapt children's story time programs to work with these teens. While one librarian is responsible for the program at the Upper Arlington Public Library in Ohio, several library staff members share the responsibility for providing programming for students with multiple disabilities at the Foothills Branch Library in Glendale, Arizona.

Library Services for Teens with Special Needs

Upper Arlington (Ohio) Public Library

Target Audience

Middle school students with special needs

Program Description

On the first and third Thursday of each month a group of young adults from the Hastings Middle School multiple disabilities class listen to stories, use computer programs, and look for reading material in the YA area of the Upper Arlington (Ohio) Public Library (UAPL). The visits were planned to provide the teens with socialization opportunities, library instruction, reader's advisory, curriculum support, and a reading session. The program was designed as a collaborative effort between the multiple disabilities teacher and the YA librarian of the public library. The goal was to introduce the students to the public library and for them to develop a comfort level with the surroundings, the staff, and other patrons. The outcome has met the goals of the school and library. The young adults have become involved in YA programs, including book discussion groups, the Volunteen program, the summer reading club, shadowing the YA librarian, and ultimately becoming independent library patrons.

Sponsoring Institution

UAPL is located in a suburb of Columbus, Ohio. It is a medium-sized municipal public library system, one of seven district libraries in Franklin County. A portion of the Library and Local Government Support Fund, which is collected and disbursed at the county level, goes to the library. Therefore, by law, UAPL must serve all state residents on an equal basis.

The UAPL system is comprised of a main facility geographically located in the center of the community, and two branches. The library system serves a city population of approximately 34,000; the overall county population is approximately 1 million. UAPL had 60,000 cardholders and a circulation of 1.5 million in 2002. The city of Upper Arlington has a population of almost five thousand young adults ranging in age from ten to nineteen years. The census of the district middle schools and high school is 3,294 students.

Young Adult Demographics

There are 142 special needs students in Upper Arlington public middle schools. The racial makeup of the community as a whole is 94.7 percent Caucasian, 3.5 percent Asian, and 0.6 percent African-American; 21.8 percent of households earn between $50,000 and $74,999, 14.9 percent earn between $75,000 and $99,999, and 16.6 percent of households earn between $100,000 and $149,999.

Program Participants

The participating students are in a multi-disabilities class at Hastings Middle School in Upper Arlington. The class size averages six students, ranging in age from twelve to sixteen years old. There are three aides and a teacher who accompany the class to the library. The students have developmental and orthopedic handicaps and have moderate to severe special needs; some of the handicaps are profound.

Youth Participation

The students and their parents have become familiar with the library and its staff, whom they see as caring professionals. The result has been the teens' participation in young adult programs, book discussion groups, and summer reading club as well as volunteer service in the library's Volunteen program. Over the years, some of the students have chosen the young adult department to shadow a staff member for their school career day—what a compliment! The teens often stop in to the library as they continue through school, most times to say "Hi," and let library staff know what they are doing. For some, this has continued well beyond their teen years; library staff members often have the pleasure of interacting with them as independent library patrons.

Staff and Volunteers

There are three aides and a teacher who accompany the class to the library. Eleven years ago a partnership was formed between Dawn Wendorff, a multi-disabilities teacher, and Betty Sheridan, the UAPL young adult librarian.

In addition to coordinating the library visits, the young adult librarian has also developed special programs for multi-disabilities students who are now in high school. One such program was Safe Internet Use, because a few of the students had visited chat rooms online. The students needed instruction that was developmentally appropriate. It took time and a creative approach to convey the concept of friend and stranger and other safety issues. This instruction is offered to the library's entire service population, but is crucial for those most vulnerable and easily deceived. The library staff was awarded the Safety: Community Service Award for our work with students and parents on safe, informed use of the Internet.

Budget

The costs of this program are included within the library and school budgets. The library services offered are ones that are available to all users, and the school transports the students to the library in teacher-driven school vans during regular class hours.

Evaluation

Although multi-disabilities students may require some adaptations in instruction and program participation, their involvement brings a depth and diversity to the library environment. The whole community benefits from their involvement in library activities. This program is a win-win situation. It has brought out the best in the library staff and has brought these students needs to the forefront.

The coordinating teacher and librarian communicate on a regular basis to make sure they are achieving the goals and meeting the needs of the students. The degree of the students' disabilities does limit their participation in planning, implementing, and evaluating the program. But the longevity of the program and the enthusiasm of the participants at all levels certainly is a testament to its success. The teachers and library staff are always checking to make sure the program is working for the teens and meeting anticipated goals. The smiles on the teens' faces tell us they enjoy the time they spend at the library.

Impact of the Program

How often have you brainstormed for ways to reach underserved teens and get them into the library and involved in programming? YALSA's *Young Adults Deserve the Best: Competencies for Librarians Serving Young Adults* (available at www.ala.org/ala/yalsa/professsionaldev/youngadultsdeserve.htm) clearly states that as young adult services providers we must "encourage teens to become lifelong library users and help them discover what libraries have to offer, in addition to identify special needs groups and design and implement programs and collections appropriate to meet their needs." Through a collaborative partnership with Hastings Middle School, the library found a way to reach an often times invisible, underserved segment of our population.

Two afternoons each month, a small group of multi-disabled teens from Hastings Middle School are transported by school van to the UAPL young adult/youth services department to interact with the library staff, listen to stories, use computer programs, and look for reading material with the help of the young adult library staff. A collaborative program was designed and developed through the summer to be implemented in the fall of the following school year, when the multi-disabilities class would be relocated to Hastings Middle School. The Upper Arlington School District has a history of excellent school libraries staffed by certified media specialists. This certainly is a wonderful advantage for the students in school, but does not provide for their library needs after school hours or as they progress as independent learners.

The primary goal of the multi-disabilities teacher was to have the students come to the library for socialization and interaction with the staff and other library patrons. Library staff were anxious to have the students involved at the library so they would feel comfortable using the facility, participate in programming, get to know the staff, and, ultimately, become lifelong library patrons. The coordinating librarian and teacher worked together to gear adapt in-library programs to dovetail with the teacher's lesson plans. Teacher collections of materials to be used in the classroom on both specific and general subjects to support the curriculum are also developed by the library. Library staff read stories aloud and then provide readers advisory for each student, helping them find material to support their educational and recreational needs. Instruction on using the library is geared towards the developmental parameters of the students so they will feel as comfortable as possible at the library. The teacher uses this time to reinforce appropriate social skills and behavior when the teens interact with staff, patrons, and fellow students. Once a year, the young adult librarian visits the students at their school to get a tour of their classroom and school, an empowering experience for them.

This program takes time to design, develop, and implement but does not require additional staff or funding. The young adult librarian happened to have previous experience with special needs students, but the only thing needed for the success of this program is a caring professional who is respectful of all patrons; who can see the unique talents and gifts of every person they serve and is committed to meeting the needs of all patrons to the best of his or her ability. The students' teacher as a partner is always the best resource and source of support on how to meet the needs of her class.

Through this program, it has become clear that special needs students are limited in their interactions with people outside their immediate family and school environment. It is essential that librarians appreciate and invite those with differences to participate in the services that our community has to offer. The library is a prime example of a resource for all to use and enjoy. This program has at times made inspired library staff to reach beyond their comfort zone, but what a rewarding reach it has been.

Students who are wheelchair-bound, have deficiencies in their communicative skills, or who process information at a slower or diminished level need the library staff to be flexible and attentive to their needs and adapt library services to accommodate specific developmental levels. It is very important for the library population, staff, and patrons to interact with this uniquely talented and gifted group of young adults. They bring with them all the fears, frustrations, and joys of being teenagers. Like all teens they try to fit in and be treated like everyone else. Working with students with multiple disabilities is both challenging and demanding, but in exchange for hard work, library staff members get to interact with teens who are delightful, engaging, and appreciative of the services offered. Serving teens with special needs is one of the most rewarding aspects of young adult library work.

For More Information

Betty Sheridan
Young Adult Librarian
2800 Tremont Rd.
Upper Arlington, OH 43221
(614) 486-9621
(614) 486-4530 (fax)
bsheridan@ualibrary.org

Teen Time Special

Foothills Branch Library, Glendale, Ariz.

Target Audience

Senior high special needs students

Program Description

This program serves high school special education classes from September to May. The library provides a revved-up storytime that, despite a more sophisticated agenda and a curriculum component, still relies heavily on picture books. Fables and fairy tales have been presented, and biographies were introduced with the life and career of Bill Peet. Another program examined illustrators' styles, and, after learning about the poured paper techniques of Denise Fleming, students tried their hands at papermaking. Focusing on individual countries has permitted the introduction of atlases and the nonfiction collection. After reading Indonesian folktales, students used crayons and tempera paint to create their own batik postcards. Information about the state of Arizona was presented through flannel board stories, interactive songs, storytelling of historical events, and reading books by such local authors as Susan Lowell. Our regular story time weekly themes are successfully adapted to fit the needs of these special teens.

Sponsoring Institution

The Foothills Branch Library (FBL) serves a diverse ethnic community in northern Glendale, Arizona. The library is a service-oriented organization whose primary responsibility is to provide free and equal access to educational, informational, recreational, and cultural resources to every man, woman, and child in the community.

Young Adult Demographics

The City of Glendale estimates its population at 225,000. About 16 percent of that population is comprised of teenagers. The three libraries in the Glendale Public Library System each serve a different segment of the city's schools, with FBL responsible for outreach and service to four middle and three high schools.

Program Participants

Teen Time Special is offered to middle and high school

special education classes. Participants exhibit varying levels of ability, and the program leaders attempt to tailor the materials and information to each group. Approximately forty-five to fifty teens participate in these programs on an ongoing basis.

Youth Participation

Because this program is so interactive, the students' participation has been vital to the enthusiasm that the program generates. Their evaluations have consisted of verbal responses at the end of each program to such questions as, "What did you learn?" and "Did you have fun?"

Staff and Volunteers

One librarian or library assistant conducts each program.

Budget

The minimal funding required for this program has come from the library's general operating budget. The costliest portion has been staff time, and even that is deceptive, as this program uses much of the material that has already been developed for children's story hours. Although preparation time varies, and the sessions usually run about forty-five minutes in length, approximately one and a half hours are required to prepare and present this program. Based on an average salary of $20 per hour, each session would cost $30.

Evaluation

The students and adults who attend the program often provide positive feedback on their experience.

Impact of the Program

This program was started with a librarian who had worked with special education students. While she acted as the initial facilitator, the library quickly decided to rotate the program among all the librarians and library assistants so that everyone would get a chance to work with these special patrons. Some staff were a bit hesitant—not sure of what to expect or how to pitch the stories at the right level. Staff members provided feedback to one another, and they have continued to use this form of self-evaluation. It can sometimes be disconcerting to encounter vocalizations, facial and verbal tics, and sleeping during a story time program. However, some of the students who appear to be the least involved are often the most profoundly affected by the program experience.

Staff has learned to relate in a comfortable manner to the students as they got to know them individually and as a group. Within the context of a structured program, where the librarian or library assistant is in charge, staff members have been able to relax as they hone their group skills and become more comfortable with this lively and enthusiastic audience.

Teen Time Special is important to teens because they can visit the library for a positive, entertaining, and educational experience during the school day. As Lea Emptage, a teaching assistant put it, "The kids' ability to learn from books is not related to their disabilities or their inabilities." The students get to know the librarians by name, and the librarians get to know them as well. The library provides a warm welcome and fun-filled, book-based programs.

Since beginning this community-based instructional program, a number of group home residents and respite care participants have joined us as patrons. Several of these groups drive past other libraries to visit FBL because we have become so genuinely enthusiastic about serving not just individuals with disabilities, but groups as well.

For More Information

Karen-Marie Allen
Youth Reference Supervisor
Foothills Branch Library
19055 N. 57th Ave.
Glendale, AZ 85308
(623) 930-3869
(623) 930-3855 (fax)
kmallen@glendaleaz.com

Index

Author Biography

Renée Vaillancourt McGrath is a freelance library consultant and feature editor of *Public Libraries* magazine, the journal of the Public Library Association. She also occasionally substitutes for the host of a children's radio program on Montana Public Radio. As a YALSA Serving the Underserved trainer, she has conducted dozens of workshops on topics related to young adult services across the Unites States. She is the author of *Managing Young Adult Services* (Neal-Schuman, 2002) and *Bare Bones Young Adult Services* (ALA, 2000) as well as numerous articles on working with teens in libraries.

McGrath has worked as a consulting acquisitions editor for ALA Editions as well as serving as a children's and young adult librarian, Access Center librarian (serving people with disabilities), and assistant director of public libraries in Rhode Island, Massachusetts, Indiana, and Montana. She obtained her MSLS from the Catholic University of America in 1993 with a Department of Education Title IIB Scholarship for Young Adult Services.

Notes

Notes

Notes